james reaney

MW00988557

listen
to
the
wind

Talonbooks
Vancouver
Los Angeles
1972

published with assistance from the Canada Council

Talonbooks   Talonbooks
201 1019 East Cordova   P.O. Box 42720
Vancouver   Los Angeles
British Columbia V6A 1M8   California 90042
Canada   U.S.A.

This book was typeset by Linda Gilbert, designed by
David Robinson and printed by Webcom for Talonbooks.

Fourth printing: April 1980

Talonplays are edited by Peter Hay.

Rights to produce *Listen to the Wind*, in whole or in part,
in any medium by any group, amateur or professional, are
retained by the author and interested persons are requested
to apply to his agent, Sybil Hutchinson, Apt. 409, Ramsden
Place, 50 Hillsboro Avenue, Toronto, Ontario M5R 1S8.

Jay Macpherson's *Introduction* is reprinted with permission
from a review of the play that appeared in *The Canadian
Forum*, September, 1966. Permission to draw upon the
names of the characters and events that were used in *Dawn*,
a novel by Rider Haggard, have been granted by the literary
executors of his estate, A.P. Watt & Son, 26/28 Bedford
Row, London WC1, England.

Canadian Cataloguing in Publication Data

Reaney, James, 1926—
    Listen to the wind

    A play.
    ISBN 0-88922-002-6 pa.

    I. Title.
    PS8535.E25L5   C812'.54   C72-5498
    PR9199.3.R42L5

introduction

Branwell Brontë at twenty-two, his literally fabulous childhood behind him, wrote in a despondent letter, ". . . nothing
to listen to except the wind." James Reaney, who in *A Suit of
Nettles* made "Branwell" the persona of a melancholy mar-
tyred poet-soul, calls his new play, written for the Summer
Theatre company in London, *Listen to the Wind*. The play,
directed by the author and performed July 26th to 29th, 1966,
was an extraordinary theatrical experience. First, its structure
of play within play. In the author's words, quoted from the
program: "In a Perth County farmhouse some time during the
thirties, a boy named Owen decides to spend the summer put-
ting on plays with the help of his cousins, his grownup relatives
and the neighborhood children. One of the plays they put on
is their adaptation of a Victorian novel, *The Saga of Caresfoot
Court*. We watch a double story: Owen fighting illness and
trying to get his parents together again; Angela Caresfoot
threading her way through a world of evil manorhouses and
sinister Lady Eldreds. The two stories illuminate each other."
They do so through numerous cross-references in image and
situation, and through the revelation of the capacities of
characters of the outer story by the roles they play in the
inner one. Further, their interlocking provides a satisfying
emotional balance. While the outer story is slight, gentle, and

3

touching, the inner one consists of a series of explosive confrontations, which unlike the outer events, are distanced from us by the conventions of English landed-gentry setting and melodramatic plot mechanics. And while the outer story runs its course over a summer, in the melodrama the other three seasons are powerfully evoked. The balance of the two stories conveys the relationship between life and creative dream. The sick boy Owen, as his physical life runs out, projects his energies in the world of the inner play, which moreover is designed as a device to bring his runaway mother back to him. To emphasize the creative power of the dream, the inner story has alternative endings, one tragic and the other happy, and the outer story breaks off before the expected death of Owen, leaving open just a hint of the possibility that the elements of real life have perhaps really been rearranged — that, following the death of a substitute victim in the offered tragic ending, there is no more short straw left to be drawn.

Next, the style, which in this play is no less substance than the plot matter. This production can fairly be taken as definitive. More money, more experienced actors, would most likely lessen its peculiar force. It is performed on a stage almost empty except for four chairs, a ladder, and a long table on which props are laid out. (In a phrase from the play, its real matter is "four children and four chairs.") On the stage at the right sit three musicians with piano, percussion, and guitar and fourteen chorus members. Most of these were high school students with a few from Western. Their entirely everyday assorted shorts and tops show them to be individuals, kids from the farms of Owen's neighborhood. The music, composed or put together by the excellent teenage musicians we see on stage, and the sound effects contributed by the chorus, provide half the life and atmosphere of the play. The chorus mime, recite, sing, thump, clap, and play instruments from recorder to pop-bottle; waving antlers, they are a forest, surging and whooshing, they are the sea, holding flowers and twittering sweetly, they are a dewy English garden. When needed, they mingle on stage as party guests or a pack of starving dogs. A letter sent to London in the inner play is passed from hand to hand through the chorus to its recipient standing far right. In such ways they are not there just to comment, like most choruses, but actively push the action on. Above all, by establishing season, prevailing wind and specific atmosphere for most of the scenes, they add immensely to the play's imaginative dimension.

"Listening to the wind" is the play's image for openness to imagination; the willingness to listen is that willed passiveness in which the Spirit can move. In the world of the play, the winds of the four quarters, and with them the night wind, all have their special moods and powers. For the audience, the play's special theme of the creative use of life is made most compelling in the child's-play simplicity of the means by which its effects are achieved. The author's program notes refer to the techniques of the Peking National Opera. These are recalled where, for example, two girls stand on chairs placed back to back and separated by a length of white cloth being agitated at floor level by two more girls. The audience sees the evil Lady Geraldine facing the beautiful Angela on a bridge across a stream that rages in the cruel East Wind. But where the Peking company relies on the fantastic training and bodily control of its actors, what is astonishing in Reaney's production is the sense of play, of freedom, of creation before one's eyes. Far from being instant or impromptu theatre, every action has been carefully planned, but the whole company has contributed to its planning, particularly in the highly inventive work of the chorus. The creative effort has spread from the author to the company and from there to the audience which perhaps explains why the play makes so unusually stimulating and satisfying an evening. Such an experience for all concerned has been made possible by the policy of London's Summer Theatre and its producer Keith Turnbull, now in their third year and eager to draw writers into their plans. *Listen to the Wind* was written for them, and besides directing his play, Reaney has also been present after each performance to answer questions and listen to comments.

Something should perhaps be said about the literary materials of the play which, besides further bearing out Reaney's view that "the simpler art is, the richer it is," have their own intriguing and involving quality of primitive — meaning basic — romance. The outer plot seems to have begun in the author's mind as a play about the four young Brontës evolving their fantasy worlds within the bare walls of Haworth Parsonage. As it developed, their situation was stripped down to the "four children," still three girls and a boy, and "four chairs," or the given objects of a distinctly sparse physical world. The choice of helpful grownups recalls the Brontë setting in Owen's father, their housekeeper, Tabby, the doctor, and the village gravedigger. The symbolism of the winds seems to have been elaborated from Brontë writings, particularly stanzas of Emily's about the night-wind and the south or "thaw-wind." Most of the Brontë references have become attached to the Caresfoot melodramatic plot in the form of stanzas from Emily's and Charlotte's poems absorbed into the chorus' part and once or twice into the dialogue, and of names — that of Emily's dog, Keeper, and ones from her Gondal saga like Brenzaida or Geraldine Almeda given to the Caresfoot characters. The Caresfoot tale itself is adapted from Rider Haggard's early novel *Dawn*, one of those Victorian tales of two generations, fraticidal cousins, estates, wills, and victim-brides like, in a sense, *Wuthering Heights*. For the play, the action of *Dawn* has been simplified and mingled with some other strains and the rhetoric and poetic touches have been sharpened and focussed. Haggard's evil lady dabbles in a vague occultism; Reaney's owes allegiance to "a certain evil-winking star." Where Haggard says of Angela's birth, "another little lamp floated out on the waters of life," a lost girl in the play is figuratively the cradle on the flood that begins a new life-cycle. A malignant doll in the Caresfoot plot recalls Haggard's childhood fear of a doll he called "She-who-must-be-obeyed," later the title of his most durable creation, the witch-woman, *She*. Other strains are the children's singing-game "Green Gravel" and the northern ballad of "The Cruel Mother," each suggesting its own whole realm of verbal magic. Both appear as words sung by the chorus and shape incidents of the action. The ballad further blends with the Gondal theme of proud lady and forsaken child. There is moreover a healthy streak of familiar Stratford macabre in that the eccentric impoverished daughter selling squire dognaps for a medical school and at length, having neglected once too often to feed the inmates of its pound, is devoured by them Jezebel-style. Too, the thirties date suggest childhood remniscences of Reaney's own.

But the play is by no means a hotchpotch. The impression it makes is extraordinarily unified, and entirely unconfusing until shortly before the end when the prospect of multiple possibilities begins to open. Reaney has seized upon and developed the essential common qualities of his materials, their pathos, their passion, their elemental sensationalism, and fused them into a poetic and forceful whole that is funny, touching, even prophetic. Even for those who see in the ending a sombre close, with nothing changed and death coming for the dreamer, still there is too a promise of renewal, a fresh start. If poetry works no magic on the outward world, it can at least refresh those who share the experience, and lend a sense of — can one call it? — confederation.

Jay Macpherson
The Canadian Forum
September, 1966

Listen to the Wind was first performed at the Althouse College Auditorium in London, Ontario on July 26, 1966, with the following cast:

The Taylor Farm, 1936	Caresfoot Court, 1860	London, Ontario present day
Owen	Arthur Brenzaida	Neil McAlister
Jenny	Maria Lawry	Hilary Bates
Ann	Claudia Von Yorick	Gwen Wilson
Harriet	Angela Caresfoot	Alice Giddings
Mitch	Piers Caresfoot	Mike Fletcher
Tom	Douglas Caresfoot	Daryl Kaufman
Dr. Spettigue	Devil Caresfoot	Paul Fleck
Tabby	Martha	Chris Burt
Mr. Taylor (Father)	Sir Edward Eldred (Dr. Surrey)	Victor Hoar
Mrs. Taylor (Mother)	Geraldine (Lady Eldred)	Sheilah White
	Baby Ghost	Gabrielle De Veber
	Mr. Gleneden	Allan Stratton
	Rogue	Bob MacMillan
	Keeper	Christine De Veber
	Julia Elbe	Ellen Richardson
	A Fiddler	David Blostein

Chorus: Grant Amyot, Debby Cheung, Jo-Anne Cheung, Diane Corneil, Heather Dennison, Frances Henderson, Aldis Johnson, Harold Johnson, Mary-Lou McCausland, Bob Ormsby, Blanche Savage, Bob MacMillan, Allan Stratton, Carol Tull.

Directed by James Reaney
With poems by Charlotte and Emily Brontë
Produced by Keith Turnbull
Music by Paul Chefurka, David Blostein, Diane and Dan Leah

Listen to the Wind was also performed at Stage 2 of the Playhouse Theatre Company in Vancouver, British Columbia on January 17, 1968, with the following cast:

The Taylor Farm, 1936	Caresfoot Court, 1860	Vancouver, B.C. present day
Owen	Arthur Brenzaida	Ian McKay
Jenny	Maria Lawry	Isabel McClure
Ann	Claudia Von Yorick	Linda Sorenson
Harriet	Angela Caresfoot	Pia Shandel
Mitch	Douglas Caresfoot	Larry Benedict
Tom	Piers Carefoot	Dermot Hennelly
Dr. Spettigue	Devil Caresfoot	Jack Ammon
	Mr. Gleneden	
Tabby	Martha	Rae Brown
Mr. Taylor (Father)	Sir Edward Eldred (Dr. Surrey)	Bill Buckingham
Mrs. Taylor (Mother)	Geraldine (Lady Eldred)	Betty Phillips
	Rogue	Wayne Specht

Chorus: Colin Barnhardt, Susan Cadman, Bunny Appleby, Scott Swan, Marti Wright.

Directed by John Wright
Sets & Lighting by Jenepher Hooper
Costumes by Sue Benson
With poems by Charlotte and Emily Brontë

act one

The stage is set with a brass bed on which a boy lies reading a book. There are four chairs, a big dining room table. On stage left, a chorus of a dozen young people like the orchestra of the Peking Opera. From this chorus will come props, sound effects, mime, anything the boy who lies reading on the bed wants when he tries to dream "it" out. Partly too, this chorus represents the audience who come to watch the play within the play, The Saga of Caresfoot Court. As the house-lights go down, we are dimly aware that there are three girls in the aisles playing with a ball that passes over our heads, back and forth. They are walking down the lane to a farmhouse to stay for the summer. As they step up onto the stage, the boy rises to greet them. The ball is thrown into the chorus, one of whom retrieves it.

SCENE 1: THE ARRIVAL

OWEN:
    Harriet, Ann, Jenny, you've come for the summer.

*He greets them with a kiss or handshake depend-
ing on certain delicate instant measurements of
how they have grown up since last summer.*

HARRIET: *plays ANGELA later*
>   Owen, this is going to be the most wonderful summer
>   yet.

ANN: *plays CLAUDIA later*
>   Do you have this whole room to yourself?

OWEN:
>   Yes, it's the West Room.

JENNY: *plays MARIA later*
>   The West Room. We'll spend the whole summer here
>   putting on plays.

OWEN:
>   Harriet, your mother?

HARRIET:
>   Oh, run away on him. She can't stand grandmother.
>   She's working up at the orphanage. But back together
>   in the fall I expect.

OWEN:
>   And your ancestors, Ann?

ANN:
>   Mother lost the baby, poor little dear. She's very ill.
>   We've all been packed off.

OWEN:
>   And you, Jenny?

JENNY:
>   Together as can be, Owen. What about you?

OWEN: *taking out a clay pipe and lighting it*
>   Mother's run off on Dad I'm afraid. She simply rode

off and said she couldn't stand us any longer. She rode
off on Dad's best horse too.

HARRIET:
Not the Electric Eel.

OWEN:
No, no. That one died. So . . .

ANN:
You're smoking a pipe?!

OWEN:
Yes, the doctor says I have to smoke it for my nerves.
Here's the tobacco. Heavy Trinidad Tobacco.

HARRIET:
Have to take it for the . . . Your nerves. Oh my, I wish
I were nervous. Here, can I have a try?

*They all have a try, some gasping and choking.
He resumes the pipe with the air of being very
much ahead of them.*

JENNY: *coughing*
At this rate Owen, you'll be getting married soon
I suspect. Do you miss your ma much?

OWEN: *nodding*
I was thinking . . . If we put on something she might
come back to see it.

HARRIET:
Where is she?

OWEN:
Just over at his place over there. You see, he'll take her
away in the fall. And . . . I want to see her again.
Mother loves plays.

HARRIET:

Well, if I were your father I'd go over to him and beat him up and drag her back. By the neck.

OWEN:

Father agrees with you. But he says . . . He says he just hasn't got the temperament for it. He would like the horse back though.

HARRIET:

He would like the horse back though. Oh.

OWEN:

What'll we put on? We could put on Tarzan of the Apes. Tarzan jad guru! Hotan woten madzewk! It's a special language he learns in this lost country. There's a glossary in the back. Harriet, you be Lady Jane Greystoke.

HARRIET:

Do come off the table, Tarzan.

OWEN has leapt up on the table.

JENNY:

Who am I to be?

OWEN:

He utters a bloodcurdling cry in the Stygian night.

HARRIET:

You're to be his female ape consort . . . Kalee. His first love. Don't you remember?

JENNY:

And who am I?

HARRIET:

You could be Mad Bertha, the German missionary lady who's really a German general in disguise trying to blow up our ammo dump in Dar es Salaam.

JENNY: *machine-gunning him*
Ja wohl. Achtung. Tarzan. Ich haben sie gefunden.

OWEN:
Tarzan leaps upon the stunned wildebeest, tears at the creature's jugular vein, then utters the wild ape's victory cry.

ANN:
Too many female apes for me. Come on, let's think of something else. Something where we can dress up in old clothes from the attic . . . Six people die in bed . . . from broken hearts . . . or poison . . . or get betrayed . . . That sort of thing.

OWEN: *producing a book*
Would you like to try this? I've been reading it all spring.

HARRIET:
Oh I've read this. "The Saga of Caresfoot Court."

ANN: *taking the book*
That dreadful part where the dog gets him by the throat at the well. And they can't get the dog's jaws loose so they bury them together.

JENNY:
And that awful part where she thinks she's poisoning herself but actually she only gets paralyzed from the waist down. Could I have that part, Owen? Owen?

HARRIET:
Terribly melodramatic. Could I play that part, Owen?

OWEN:
What's melodramatic?

HARRIET:
Oh I don't know . . . But I want to do the poisoning scene.

JENNY:

    I want it.

OWEN:

    There's someone else I've got in mind.

HARRIET:

    Who?

ANN:

    Your father gave this to your mother before they got married, didn't he?

OWEN:

    Yes. You know as I've been reading it here . . . Sometimes I feel I don't really live or die here in Ontario, but I lived a century ago in an old manorhouse in England . . . With the rain beating down on the window . . . And the wind whistling around the eaves.

ANN:

    How does it begin, Owen?

HARRIET:

    A funny old Victorian novel. Can we wear old dresses? Lots of good parts for girls.

OWEN:

    No parts at the beginning for girls. There's a quarrel between two brothers. An angry old father intercepts. This can be the haunted well down in front of the manor house.

JENNY:

    The cellar trap door.

OWEN:

    I can almost see them as I lie here and . . .

SCENE 2: THE FOUR WINDS

CHORUS:
>Listen to the Wind!

OWEN:
>Let's hear the North Wind.

>*The chorus imitate it.*

>The South Wind? The West Wind that brings the Evening Star.

>*As before.*

>The Night Wind. The East Wind.

CHORUS:
>Once there were four children who listened to the wind:
>Jenny, Owen, Harriet, and Ann.
>Weathervane, weathervane, the Northwest Wind,
>Like a hound the smoke leaps after the wind
>As we sit by the fire and hear the rushing sound
>Of the wind that comes from Temiskaming,
>Algoma, Patricia,
>Down from the North over the wilderness
>For one purpose they come
>The fierce howling mother and the rain, her doll,
>The black huntsman and his men,
>The wind and the wild, wild rain
>To make the branch tap at my windowpane
>To cry and to tap at my windowpane.

>*A girl comes forward with a whirling weathervane and another girl carries a window against which a boy taps a branch. The chorus raise branches, maple keys flutter down, flags wave in the wind. As the branch taps at the window the chorus says:*

Tap tap tip! Tap tap tip!
Scritch scritch tap tap tip!
What are you writing on the frosty pane?
What words do you scratch on my crystal brain?

The branches wave in the wind!
Listen to the wind and the patter of the sleet
And the touch of the snow and the drum of the rain.
It lulls me awake. Keen, keen awake.
The wild, wild music wailed to me
The drear moor stretches far away.
Shall I pretend I'm the Goblin Hunter?
Look, I can make the wind sound.
Here's the sound the branches make.

Listen to the wind! Listen to the . . .

OWEN:

The North Wind!

> *He takes the weathervane pole, which is like the
> mace for an inner parliament of the soul gathered
> with Death Angels on the right and Life Angels
> on the left.*

SCENE 3: THE FIGHT

> *DOUGLAS and PIERS are about to come up the
> aisle.*

HARRIET:

Piers is the rightful heir. Oh, you've got that boy who
takes care of the church.

ANN:

Douglas is . . . No one knows who his father is. Where
do they live?

OWEN:

At Caresfoot Court. These four chairs can be the house.

JENNY:

This is the old tree that grows by the house.

OWEN: *arranging it*

A stepladder. Yes.

HARRIET:

In summer its shadow falls down into the haunted well at its foot.

OWEN:

Listen!

> *They retire to the edge of the stage as PIERS and DOUGLAS come down the aisles quarrelling across a section of audience.*
>
> *PIERS is played by MITCH, the caretaker of the church close by. DOUGLAS is played by TOM, a neighbour's boy. DEVIL CARESFOOT is played by the family doctor who glides out and hides behind the tree, turning his back to us. The fight occurs at the well.*

PIERS:

You're lying, Douglas. You told father about the money I got for the rabbit skins.

DOUGLAS: *played by TOM*

But I caught the rabbits and you were supposed to give me some of the money but you never did. When your father asked me I was so scared I told him. Piers, you forgot I'm not your father's son. He can boot me out any time he likes.

PIERS:

You told him so I'd get kicked out. You want to play cowbird, don't you? Squeeze me out of my own nest.

DOUGLAS:

Piers, I don't. If you'd have given me the money I worked for, but you're tighter than a barn door.

PIERS:

What do you need money for? Who bought the traps and whose ferret is it?

DOUGLAS:

I want to buy something for my girl.

PIERS:

Well lay off that gypsy slut and forget about your money for a while. If only the old man weren't such a skinflint. We can eat off gold plate but I have to scour the countryside for money of my own.

DOUGLAS:

Why don't you hunt wild animals instead of tame ones?

PIERS:

What do you mean, Douglas?

DOUGLAS:

I know that the surgeon who runs the little medical school in Roxham has commissioned you to bring him all the stray dogs you can catch so his scholars can cut them up.

PIERS:

You're going to tell father that I suppose.

DOUGLAS:

No.

PIERS:

I'll give you something to tell him, you bastard.

> *DOUGLAS fights like a cornered rat, but he is smaller and soon falls down.*

20

Now get up, you half-bred beggar. Your tinker's daughter of a mother didn't have enough suck in her breasts to make you a fighter.

DOUGLAS moans, especially as DEVIL CARES-FOOT now appears.

DEVIL: *played by DR. SPETTIGUE*
Having a little talk with your cousin, Piers? What's the matter, Douglas? Did you fall over when Piers was talking to you?

DOUGLAS:
Don't blame Piers, Mr. Caresfoot. We were scuffling and . . .

DEVIL:
So Piers, you're a brute as well as a liar. The younger and weaker are to be knocked about, are they?

PIERS:
Father, you're turning me into a scoundrel. If you'd only trust me . . . Even with some money.

DEVIL:
But you're not to be trusted. Piers because you're forever lying.

PIERS:
You make me lie! You want me to lie!

DOUGLAS:
Pay no attention, uncle. He doesn't mean it.

DEVIL:
Then something he doesn't mean will cost him dear. Piers Carefoot, if ever I find out again that you have deceived me, by Heaven, I will disinherit you in favour of . . . Ah . . .

He falls back against the house, pressing his hands to his breast. They spring forward, but he recovers himself.

DEVIL:

Nothing. Alright. I wish you both good morning.

He exits.

PIERS:

Douglas, get out of my sight. Why does there always have to be dark you!

He exits.

DOUGLAS goes over to the girls and OWEN. PIERS leans moodily on the stepladder while OWEN and JENNY arrange the four chairs into an avenue of trees leading up to Hawkscliffe Hall. JENNY stands at the end of the avenue to receive PIERS. OWEN puts forth a staff with the Hawkscliffe symbol on it and announces:

SCENE 4: HAWKSCLIFFE HALL

OWEN:

Down the avenue of beech trees that led to Hawkscliffe Hall . . .

ANN:

Piers walked to see his friend, Maria Lawry.

PIERS:

Maria, my cousin Douglas has wound father round his servant fingers. Father always favours him.

MARIA: *played by JENNY*
>Poor Piers, you're not treated well but I don't like
>your beating up Douglas nor your holding back his
>rabbit skin money.

PIERS:
>I know. You see, I can't control myself. He knew
>I'd hit him in front of father. It was mean, I'll admit.

MARIA:
>Piers, if you get into trouble again tell me first before
>you do anything foolish.

PIERS:
>Maria, you're the only friend I have. May I kiss you?

MARIA:
>Certainly not. Well, if you really want to. Now I'll
>walk you out to the end of the beeches.

SCENE 5: FAREWELL FATHER

OWEN: *with the Caresfoot symbol on a staff*
>Caresfoot Court.

>*The girls quickly arrange the four chairs back
>into the Caresfoot Court facade. PIERS returns to
>find DEVIL CARESFOOT waiting for him by
>the well.*

DEVIL:
>May I ask what delayed you, Piers?

PIERS:
>I was over talking to Miss Lawry, father.

DEVIL:

> Oh. Piers, I commend your taste. Miss Lawry is the heiress to some fine old meadows.

PIERS:

> Why is this old tree called Caresfoot Staff?

DEVIL:

> The first Caresfoot was a swineherd in this forest, Piers. One day he saved a great acorn big as an egg from the pigs' sharp teeth and he planted it by the well here. It's been known as Caresfoot Staff ever since. That was 300 years ago, Piers. Piers, the Michaelmas term at college begins next week. I put you down on their list years ago and I want you to go and get your rough edges smoothed off.

PIERS:

> Is he to go too?

DEVIL:

> Douglas? No. He shall be my forester, my game-keeper and huntsman. I shall not try to polish him up.

PIERS:

> But he'll be here all the time while I'm away.

DEVIL:

> You are my son, Piers. Douglas is not. He has wild, brutish tastes. Yesterday I caught him embracing one of the Charlatan's daughters, the gyspy girl, who lives with her father on the common. Poor rascal. He has nothing better to do of course.

PIERS:

> You would not forgive me if you caught me embracing her, father?

DEVIL:

> No. Because you are made of finer stuff. You are *my* son, Piers. Touch the old tree by the haunted well.

You will hold the yeoman's staff one day. Be like it, of an oaken English heart and you will defy wind and weather as it has done. And there will always be Caresfoots beneath your branches as Caresfoot Court.

SCENE 6: THE GROWNUPS

CHORUS:
Listen to the Wind! Once there were four grownups who helped the four children listen to the wind.

The doctor, the father, the housekeeper and the young sexton come forward, turn to the audience and raise their hands when the chorus mentions them.

There was Tabby, the old housekeeper and nurse.

She goes over to the children and confides.

TABBY:
And do you know, Owen, Harriet, Jenny and Ann, that although both mother and daughter have long mouldered in their graves, you may still see them at night walking and weeping in the garden.

TABBY goes back to her bench.

CHORUS:
There was the boy's father whose father had raised horses for a living.

OWEN lies down in the bed and his father goes over to him.

FATHER:
You look well today, old man.

25

OWEN:
>Do I, father?

FATHER:
>You've got someone to play with. My God, they've got good appetites though. They'll eat me out of home and barn.

OWEN:
>Feed them out of my garden then.

FATHER: *laughing*
>Your garden's not up yet, Owen. I was just joking, old man. Just joking.

>*He goes back to the grownups' bench.*

CHORUS:
>There was the doctor who came to see the boy almost daily.

>*The doctor in the beard he wears for the Devil Caresfoot part goes over to OWEN.*

DOCTOR:
>Owen.

OWEN:
>Doctor.

>*He feels the Doctor's beard.*

>Thank you, Dr. Spettigue. Every inch that beard grows I feel more alive.

DOCTOR:
>I'll have to shave it off some day, Owen.

OWEN:
>Sure, someday, Dr. Spettigue. When?

DOCTOR:
>Owen, here's your pipe. Light it. Relax yourself.
When it comes you'll never know it has come.
It may never come. What you must do is live.

>*The doctor departs.*

>Remember now, live. Your cousins have come to
play with you. Put on your play, I'll help you. Dream
it out, as you say. Dream it out, Owen.

OWEN:
>Mitch. Come in and talk to me, Mitch. What grave
are you digging today?

CHORUS:
>And there was the young man who took care of the
church next to the house where the children listened
to the wind.

MITCH: *with spade and boots*
>Hi, Owen. Burying old Mrs. Hoffmeyer, the saf.
You can watch the funeral out the window if you
like.

OWEN:
>Tell me something that will freeze my marrow and
chill my bones.

MITCH:
>Well there was this man buried alive, Mr. Owen. Poor
bugger. We'd buried him alive.

>*He mimes this.*

>*OWEN laughs and shivers.*

>*An owl cries.*

>*We hear galloping horse hooves.*

CHORUS:

>She sat down below a thorn
>Fine flowers in the valley
>And there she has her sweet babe
>And the green leaves they grow rarely.

TABBY:

>When she was seventeen she married him. Her father paid him to marry her. Oh, he used her awful rough. When she turned eighteen why, she came home to die.

CHORUS:

>Why do I hate that lone green dell
>Buried in moors and mountains wild?
>
>I dream of moor and misty hill
>Where evening gathers, dark and chill.

SCENE 7: AT THE EDGE OF THE FOREST

>*One of the chorus runs across the stage with a pair of antlers in his hands. ANN takes Geraldine's part for the moment, stands beneath the stepladder waiting for DOUGLAS who dismounts from the horse (table) and advances through the chorus (thicket) towards GERALD-INE. He bears letters in his hand.*
>
>*Beneath a tree the pale faced woman waits as DOUGLAS dismounts from his horse and comes toward her.*

DOUGLAS:

>Geraldine, I've come to ask you the meaning of these letters.

GERALDINE: *played by ANN temporarily*

> Attorney Eldred wants to marry me, Douglas. He's mad for me. I can't wait any longer for you to come to something.

DOUGLAS:

> How are you going to explain our baby to Eldred? In this last infernal letter you say . . . By God, I refuse to read that again.

GERALDINE:

> I'm not going to explain it to him.

DOUGLAS:

> What do you mean?

GERALDINE:

> Douglas, I'm tired of living at the edge of a forest like a gypsy. I want to get inside their houses and eat their white bread and drink their red wine and wear their gold rings. And I shall. Our baby has to go! Douglas, there is within me a spirit of power that I've always known was mine ever since I helped my father with his mesmerism. That spirit, Douglas, is a river in jail as things now stand. You'll be a gamekeeper the rest of your life, Douglas. I've killed our baby.

DOUGLAS:

> Your letter says that, I see now. I see now what you meant.

GERALDINE:

> It was in the way, Douglas. Why if I marry Eldred, I'll be able to help you far more than now. I'll always be yours.

DOUGLAS:

> You have murdered a part of me.

GERALDINE:

> What does it matter?

DOUGLAS:

Couldn't you trust me? Couldn't you wait?

GERALDINE:

I bring you all the more love. I killed it for your sake,
Douglas.

DOUGLAS:

No, Geraldine, you've used me infernally. By God,
you shall pay for this.

GERALDINE:

I was afraid of this. I thought my writing to you
would prepare you but instead . . .

DOUGLAS:

And so you want these letters back?

He drops them and then stamps on them.

GERALDINE:

Oh Douglas, yes!

DOUGLAS:

No, Geraldine. I'm not going to give them back. It's
not wise to have you loose in the world without a rope
around your neck.

GERALDINE:

Please, Douglas.

DOUGLAS:

May you never bear another child.

GERALDINE:

I never hope to.

DOUGLAS:

Still love me, Geraldine?

GERALDINE:
Yes.

OWEN:
Just a moment, Ann and Tom. Do you see who's coming in the lane. It's my mother.

He flies out into the audience to meet her near the back of the auditorium.

Mother!

MOTHER:
Owen, should you be running so hard and so fast?

OWEN:
You've come at last.

MOTHER:
I saw the posters for the play. I couldn't miss that.

OWEN:
Where's your horse?

MOTHER:
I left him at the blacksmith's shop. Listen, you can hear them working on his shoes.

Anvil distant tink tink from the chorus.

My son.

They embrace.

OWEN:
Can you be Geraldine in the play, mother?

MOTHER:
Why of course I can. What part are you at?

OWEN:
>   We're at the scene where she meets Douglas at the edge
>   of the forest and has to explain that . . .

>   *Back to back ANN and mother whirl around until*
>   *ANN is spun off and mother takes over the*
>   *Geraldine part.*

DOUGLAS:
>   May you never bear another child.

GERALDINE: *now played by MRS. TAYLOR*
>   I never hope to.

DOUGLAS:
>   Still love me, Geraldine?

GERALDINE:
>   Yes.

DOUGLAS:
>   The ground's rather muddy hereabouts and I want to
>   keep the mud off these good boots of mine. Come,
>   Geraldine.

>   *She kneels down and cleans off his boots with a*
>   *twig.*

>   I wonder if Attorney Eldred ever thought he'd be
>   marrying a child murderess. Some day he might like
>   to know.

>   *She listens as his horse gallops off.*

BABY GHOST:
>   So you killed me for nothing, mother.

GERALDINE:
>   Oh my sweet babe, my first little child with golden
>   hair. If you were alive now I'd clothe you in silk.

GHOST:

When I lived you weren't so kind to me. You farmed me out with the woodcutter's old woman and she never cleaned her milk pan, all buzzing with flies and stink.

GERALDINE:

Oh my bonny child, if you knew the rusty arrow that sticks in my breast.

GHOST:

The rusty penknife in mine.

GERALDINE:

What must I do to be free of this?

GHOST:

You'll be seven long years a wolf in the woods.

GERALDINE:

A wolf from the woods is what I shall be. God help the deer whose throat I catch my teeth in.

Fades away.

SCENE 8: YEARS LATER, ANN

ANN comes forward pensively, close to the chorus.

CHORUS:

What are you thinking of, Miss Wilson?

ANN:

I was thinking of home and the games we children played there.

CHORUS:
> What games?

ANN:
> Dreaming it out. Imagining. My cousin and I used to
> call it "the world below" which we can enter when-
> ever we are alone or . . . Listening to the wind. And in
> the world below why, all is as we see it. Four children
> and four chairs. We make up stories about Douglas,
> the Goblin Hunter, and a kingdom called Caresfoot
> Court, and an old tree by a haunted well.

CHORUS:
> Miss Wilson, Miss Wooler says that it is time that you
> came and helped the kindergarten on with their
> snowsuits.

> *ANN exits.*

SCENE 9: THE RAILWAY STATION

JENNY:
> Owen, how do we do this part? It says . . . You say
> that . . . I drive to the station in a carriage. I don't
> think your father's going to let you bring even a pony
> right up the stairs and into this room.

OWEN:
> Ah. Instead of the carriage or the coach or the . . .
> We have one of its four wheels.

> *A neighbour boy brings over a wheel from the
> prop table.*

34

Now Bob, you'll have to be the horse and roll the wheel along beside you.

> *BOB does this, kicking up his heels in a demonstration.*

This was a carriage. Let's see a lumber wagon going up a hill.

> *BOB illustrates this.*

Now Jenny, walk over to the carriage and step into it. When you're *in* the carriage, you run as fast as Bob does, but outside of the carriage you . . .

> *As the "carriage" journeys with MARIA to the station it should go on a journey that takes in part of the auditorium so that the boy running with the wheel "enchants" itself into the onlookers' minds. In the original production this mime seemed to sum up the play. DEVIL CARESFOOT limps over to the "carriage," but once "in" it, he runs like a boy. The various journeys can also have various "distance" conventions: for example, a physicist who watched the play remarked that the places farthest away had the shortest trips.*

> *JENNY leaves Hawkscliffe Hall for the station which is suggested by OWEN holding up a crossbuck. CLAUDIA (ANN) and PIERS (MITCH) arrive on a train perhaps pushed by a member of the chorus on a low trolley.*

MARIA:
> Piers, this is a surprise. What are you doing travelling on a second class carriage?

PIERS:
> Well, it saves money Maria. But how did you know I would be coming home on this train?

MARIA:

I didn't. I've really come to meet Claudia. She's a dear sweet girl I met abroad and she's poor and wants to learn English so she can go back and teach in Denmark. She's to be my companion. Isn't she lovely?

CLAUDIA advances carrying her luggage.

PIERS:

Maria, I've another surprise for you. Miss Von Yorick and I have already introduced ourselves on the train.

MARIA:

Then I shall save my breath and bid you all get into my carriage. Your father will be anxious to see you today but tomorrow, Piers, you must come to lunch with us at Hawkscliffe.

They drive off, PIERS separating to play the next scene with his father.

SCENE 10: HOME AGAIN

OWEN:

Caresfoot Court.

DEVIL:

Piers, welcome home. You've come back to take your proper place and soon you'll take it too.

PIERS:

You mustn't talk of dying yet, father.

DEVIL:

My life hangs on a thread. You see that cupboard? Open it. Take out that bottle. Now, Piers, if ever you see me taken with an attack of the heart, you

run for that as hard as you can go. The doctor says
if I don't take it when the next attack comes, there'll
be an end of Devil Caresfoot.

PIERS:
Yes, father.

DEVIL:
Another thing. Get married. Before I die I want to
see grandchildren. Why not marry Maria Lawry.
Good plain girl. Besides her property would put yours
into a ring fence. Think that over, Piers.

PIERS:
Father, I have thought it over. But perhaps she'll not
have me.

DEVIL:
Go over and see her. She's come back from abroad
I hear. Don't be afraid, Piers. She'll have you,
my boy.

SCENE 11: GARDEN PARTY

OWEN:
Hawkscliffe Hall.

> *The chairs are arranged to illustrate the avenue,
> then carried off to reveal the scene.*

DOUGLAS: *to PIERS entering*
How are you, Piers? You're back from college.

PIERS:
Hello, Douglas. Who on earth let you in?

> *PIERS, DOUGLAS and SIR EDWARD (father)
> on stage right. GERALDINE, MARIA and*

*CLAUDIA over by the chorus. The chorus
represent the garden and can hold up some lilies.*

DOUGLAS:
> Miss Lawry. Poor Uncle. I guess you've noted how much
> he's failed. Eldred here was remarking it.

ELDRED: *played by MR. TAYLOR*
> I certainly did think, Mr. Piers, that the squire looked
> aged when I saw him yesterday.

PIERS:
> Well you see, Mr. Eldred, eighty-two is a good age,
> is it not?

ELDRED:
> Yes, Mr. Piers, a good age, a very good age, for the
> *next heir.*

DOUGLAS:
> By the way Piers, do you know Mrs. Eldred?

PIERS:
> Why Douglas, you have learned to be a gentleman
> while I've been away. I didn't know you were married,
> Mr. Eldred.

DOUGLAS:
> Ah Piers, let me introduce you to the most charming
> lady I know of, Mrs. Eldred.

> *A bow and curtsey, but MRS. ELDRED
> (Geraldine) is abstracted. She has been engaged
> in a staring match with CLAUDIA who with
> a grimace of dislike leaves the room and walks
> into the garden.*

MRS. ELDRED: *played by GERALDINE*
> She looks as if she were afraid of me. Or rather as if
> she hated me on sight. Come Eldred, we must be

going. But before I go, Mr. Caresfoot, I want to give
you a piece of advice. Make your choice pretty soon
or you will lose them both.

PIERS:

Why Mrs. Eldred, what do you mean?

MRS. ELDRED:

I mean nothing at all or just as much as you like.
And for the rest, I use my eyes. Come, let us join
the others.

PIERS follows CLAUDIA into the garden.

MRS. ELDRED:

Ah Miss Lawry, what a lovely woman your companion
is. When I am in the room with her I feel dowdy as a
milkmaid. Don't you, Miss Lawry?

MARIA:

I never thought about it, but of course she is lovely
and I am plain.

MRS. ELDRED:

I should not care to trust my admirer (*if* I had one)
for one single day in her company. Would you?

MARIA:

Why Mrs. Eldred, whatever do you mean?

In the garden.

CLAUDIA: *played by ANN*
Mr. Caresfoot, why have you come out?

PIERS:

To walk with you.

CLAUDIA:

You had better go back. They want you in the
drawing room.

PIERS:

>I will Claudia, if you promise me something. Claudia, meet me this evening at nine o'clock in the summer house?

CLAUDIA:

>Mr. Caresfoot, is not Maria in love with you? Don't you encourage her? Don't lie to me. She tells me all.

PIERS:

>Nonsense Claudia. If you'll meet me tonight I'll explain everything. You don't have to be jealous.

CLAUDIA: *stamping*
>I am not jealous and I will not meet you. I respect myself too much and you too little.

>*She exits.*

PIERS: *knocking a flower over with his stick*
>I'll give you something to be jealous about.

MARIA:

>Piers, what are you doing? That's one of my swan lilies.

PIERS:

>I'm sorry. Won't you wear it? Where are the others?

MARIA:

>They've all gone. What do you think of Mrs. Eldred?

PIERS:

>Rather the sorceress, isn't she? Where on earth did Eldred pick her up? He's such a funny toad of a fellow.

MARIA:

>I wish he hadn't picked her up. She says unpleasant things. Piers, I'm not very quick but do you know what I think Mrs. Eldred was insinuating just now?

PIERS:

>No, I didn't hear.

MARIA:

>She was trying to say that you were in love with my companion, Claudia. That's not true, is it Piers? If it's true it's better that I should know. I shan't be angry, Piers.

PIERS: *pausing*

>Maria, Claudia I admire very much but that is all. Why I always thought I was half engaged to you. I've only been waiting till I could ask if you think me worth marrying.

MARIA:

>You've made me very happy, Piers.

PIERS:

>I'm so glad you can find anything in me to like, Maria. Now could you do something for me? I want our engagement to be kept a secret. Not even your friend Claudia must know for the present.

MARIA:

>Yes Piers, I will do that for you. I trust you as much as I love you and for years I've loved you with all my heart. And now dear, please go. I want to think.

>*As he leaves a servant hands him a note from CLAUDIA.*

CLAUDIA:

>Mr. Caresfoot, I have changed my mind. I will meet you in the summer house this evening. I have something to say to you.

PIERS:

>She must stop this if I'm going to marry Maria. But I cannot bear to part with her. I love her! I love her!

SCENE 12: MOONLIT GARDEN

OWEN:

    The garden at Hawkscliffe by moonlight.

    The chairs are arranged in a summer house.
    CLAUDIA sits waiting as PIERS slowly
    approaches.

    An owl cries. Far away, a dog barks.

CLAUDIA:

    I must leave Piers, I must. I see what is going to
    happen. I, the poor paid companion, have nothing
    but my beauty. Your father would never let you
    marry me. So I will be put aside for Maria.

PIERS:

    Claudia, it's you I love.

CLAUDIA:

    Piers, my ancestors were princes of royal blood when
    yours still herded swine in the woods there. I'll not
    become your woman. I have too much pride for that.

PIERS:

    Claudia, I will marry you.

CLAUDIA:

    Think Piers. Would your father consent?

PIERS:

    God no! It would have to be a secret marriage.

CLAUDIA:

    Piers, you know how you love money. Maria is rich
    and would be a better wife for you.

PIERS:

> I . . . Love money? Why, I'd rather lose my life than lose you. I love you more than my honour or my money. When will you marry me?

CLAUDIA:

> My dearest, when you will.

PIERS:

> Then leave here as you planned, tomorrow. I'll meet you in London. We can be married and I'll rent us lodgings in Battersea.

CLAUDIA:

> Must it be a secret from everybody?

PIERS:

> Everybody. Until father dies.

CLAUDIA:

> I don't like it. But I love you so. Why Piers, up in London you will not be able to stay with me all the time . . . You'll have to come down here.

PIERS:

> It won't be for long Claudia. Father can't live much longer Claudia . . . The day after tomorrow we'll be married! My love, my life!

> *They walk off into the audience, to London and a secret marriage.*

> *The chorus now takes over the stage.*

SCENE 13: THE SOUTH WIND

The South Wind, the thaw wind
Blows the snow away.

Great white birds on the brown hills
    Smaller day by day.

Green ladies lie in the fields
    When the spring has come.
The South Wind brings them bobolinks
    And golden bees' hum.

The woods are dark with the new green leaves,
    The blossoms fall to the ground,
The small birds sing and sing and sing —
    A merry summer sound.

The bitter dark walnut trees
    Unfold their pale green flowers
So bittersweet unfold unfold
    The secret waiting hours.

Though cloudshadows darkly fly
    My heart leaps within me
The orchard bough is heavy ripe
    And the Harvest Moon I see.

Rich humming effect.

The South Wind The South Wind The South Wind

SCENE 14: THE CARRIAGE

OWEN:
    Hawkscliffe Hall.

    DEVIL CARESFOOT arrives in his carriage.
    MARIA welcomes him. Devise a wheel mime for
    the carriage, coconut shells for the hoof sounds.
    Some effect for the gravel crunch of the wheels.

DEVIL:

> Forgive an old man who has no time to waste if he comes to the point. It is now eight months since Piers came home from college. My dear Maria, it seemed so likely then . . . Is there *now* any understanding between Piers and yourself?

MARIA:

> Oh Squire Caresfoot, yes! We have been engaged for all these eight months.

DEVIL:

> Why has the affair been kept so secret?

MARIA:

> I don't know. Piers wished it so.

DEVIL:

> Maria, I am pleased to find that you love my son.

MARIA:

> I'm so glad. If I marry Piers I'll try to be a good daughter to you.

DEVIL:

> *If* you marry Piers.

MARIA:

> I say *if* because, oh Mr. Caresfoot, I have sometimes thought lately that perhaps Piers wanted to break it off.

DEVIL:

> Break it off! By God, the day he plays fast and loose with you, that day I leave the property to his cousin, Douglas. I shall have a talk with him.

> *The chairs are rapidly rearranged back into the Caresfoot Court shape.*

SCENE 15: DINNER, FATHER?

OWEN:
Caresfoot Court.

> *DEVIL CARESFOOT simply steps nearer the well and PIERS steps up to stage left of the well.*

PIERS:
Fifty people to dinner, father?

DEVIL:
Certainly. Come and help with the invitations. Now that I've got you back from London I shall put you to work. Oh it took Douglas to smoke you out. Here, write to Gunter's and order a man cook to be here on Tuesday. Write him that we expect fifty to dinner.

SCENE 16: THE FOREST HUT

OWEN:
A hut in the forest.

> *The antlers go by. DOUGLAS should have a clipboard on which he takes dictation.*

GERALDINE: *reading*
"I have changed my mind. I will meet you in the summer house this evening. I have something to say to you." Oh what beautiful handwriting. Well Douglas, we too can write. With your left hand, Douglas, scrawl the following: "A sincere friend warns Mrs. Piers Caresfoot that while she lives lonely in the great city elsewhere her husband is deceiving her

and has become entangled with a young lady of her acquaintance. *Burn this*, semicolon, wait and watch, exclamation mark!"

SCENE 17: FEAST AT CARESFOOT

The chorus take over as servants. A great white tablecloth is spread. Imaginary dishes. Carriages come up. DEVIL is at head of table. Beside him, MARIA. PIERS is at the other end. When MARIA arrives, DEVIL kisses her and most definitely makes much of her. The chorus could line up with lighted candles, some token for a festal hall.

OWEN:
Caresfoot Court.

DOUGLAS:
Piers seems very happy, doesn't he?

GERALDINE:
Believe me, he is not happy and unless I am mistaken, he will be even less happy before the night is over. We are not all asked here for nothing.

DOUGLAS:
Could this gold cup ever be mine?

GERALDINE:
Yes, if you will be guided by me.

The cloth is removed and wine is handed around. A gold cup dominates the table.

GERALDINE:
Look at your cousin's face, Douglas.

DEVIL:

My friends. My neighbours. You who have known me
as Devil Caresfoot, not without reason, will soon know
me no longer. I fall like one of the leaves from Caresfoot's Staff in autumn and I go to join the general
mould, but the bare branches will spring afresh with
green leaves because what I have to announce is my
son's engagement to Miss Maria Lawry, the young lady
on my right.

GERALDINE: *regarding Piers*
Look at his face. Look quick.

DEVIL:

You all know Miss Lawry. A sound shoot from good
old stock. Their engagement is a joy to my old age.
May God deal with my son as he deals with Maria
Lawry. I give you my toast, my only son Piers and
his affianced wife, Maria Lawry.

*After the toast the ladies withdraw with MARIA.
Eventually PIERS is left alone with his father.
They face each other down the table.*

Well Piers, how did you like my speech?

PIERS:

Father, by what authority did you announce me as
engaged to Miss Lawry?

DEVIL:

By my own, Piers. I had it from both of you
separately that you were engaged. Why should it
remain secret?

PIERS:

Father you had no right to make that speech. Understand once and for all, I will *not* marry her.

He exits.

DEVIL:

You prefer to stick to that slut you've doubtless got up in town, eh? I give you a choice, Piers. Keep your woman whoever she is and lose the land or marry Miss Lawry and keep your birthright. Oh God, all my plans come to this end. The only power left me is the power of vengeance . . . Vengeance on my own son.

SCENE 18: FOREST HUT AGAIN

OWEN:

A hut in the forest.

The antlered figure darts so we know we are in the forest.

DOUGLAS:

Well how shall we strike? I've got a copy of the marriage certificate. There's no time to lose. He might die any day.

GERALDINE:

No. We must act through her . . . Mrs. Piers . . . Claudia.

DOUGLAS:

Why?

GERALDINE:

It is more scientific and it will be more amusing.

DOUGLAS:

Don't you like her?

GERALDINE:

Once she left a room because I was in it. So I am glad now to have the chance to destroy her.

DOUGLAS:
> She's heavy with child.

GERALDINE:
> Douglas, go to town tomorrow morning and post
> this letter.

> *They retire to their bench as CLAUDIA stands
> and reads their note.*

CLAUDIA: *reading*
> "Last night Mr. Piers Caresfoot's engagement to Miss
> Maria Lawry was publicly announced at a dinner
> given at Caresfoot Court by Squire Caresfoot for
> fifty guests."

SCENE 19: THE LIBRARY

OWEN:
> The Library at Caresfoot.

> *He holds up a book.*

> *We see CLAUDIA dress and veil herself in
> London. She takes the train to Roxham. She
> takes a cab out to Caresfoot Court. The chorus
> can suggest all of this. The crossbuck and wheel
> should be used to suggest an important journey.*

DEVIL: *enters slowly and sits down*
> Whom have I the honour of addressing?

CLAUDIA: *removing her veil*
> Do you not know me, Squire Caresfoot?

DEVIL:
> Surely, yes. You're the young lady who lived with
> Maria Lawry for a while as her companion, Miss
> Claudia Von Yorick.

CLAUDIA:
> That was my name, sir. It is now Claudia Caresfoot.
> I am your son Piers' wife.

DEVIL:
> So madam. I have gotten a very lovely daughter-in-
> law. Pray take off your cloak. Hastings, take Mrs.
> Caresfoot's effect to the red room for now. You look
> rather tired and pale, Mrs. Caresfoot. Perhaps you
> might like to follow Hastings?

CLAUDIA:
> Thank you, Mr. Caresfoot. I should like to rest. But
> first I have some papers to show you.

DEVIL: *reading*
> Then you are my son's legal wife?

CLAUDIA:
> Yes. Read the anonymous notes as well, sir. I want
> to know if what they say is true.

DEVIL:
> Yes. You've married a scoundrel who happens to be
> my son. Hastings, show Mrs. Caresfoot to her room
> and see that Dr. Surrey drops by. Oh yes, I should also
> like Lawyer Eldred to come this afternoon and see me.

CLAUDIA lies down on the bed. DEVIL CARESFOOT sits in his chair. The shadows change. A clock strikes seven.

DEVIL:

>   Hello Piers. Back again, are you? That's lucky. I wanted to speak to you. Come in here please.

PIERS:

>   Alright father. But if it's all the same to you I should like to get some dinner first.

DEVIL:

>   We'll dine together presently, son. Have some wine. Oh it was here on this very table that my mother's coffin stood fifty years ago. I was standing where you are now when I wrenched off the lid to kiss her once more and last. That was a first of May, a long gone first of May. They threw branches of blackthorn blossom in upon her coffin. About Maria, Piers, you have come to a decision?

PIERS:

>   No, I have not.

DEVIL:

>   Strange. I suppose you are not already married.

PIERS:

>   Married? No, indeed. What put that idea into your head?

DEVIL:

>   Then what does this piece of paper mean? You liar. Your wife is at this moment come to this house and is big with child.

PIERS:

>   Damn her to hell then! I told her . . . She promised!

DEVIL:

>Piers, you lied to your wife, to poor Maria, and you lied to me. Hear the truth. Now while I'm alive, I disinherit you. When I'm dead, I'll haunt you if I can. Attorney Eldred helped me change the will this afternoon.

PIERS:

>Father, you want me to lie to you. For years you've wanted me to do this. Well, do your worst father. I hate you. I wish to God you were dead.

DEVIL:

>My son!

>>*Heart attack. PIERS runs for the bottle.*

>My son!

PIERS:

>Listen to me, old man. This medicine will save your life. If I let it fall, you will die and there is no more in the house. Swear before God that you'll change the will back and I will give it to you. Lift up your hand to show me that you swear or I'll pour it out before your eyes.

DEVIL:

>Murderer!

>>*DEVIL CARESFOOT dies.*

>>*PIERS smears the medicine over his mouth and breaks the glass, then pulls a bell rope.*

PIERS:

>Father. Father.

>>*Servants come and the father is laid out on the table.*

53

DR. SURREY:

Oh my old friend, gone at last. Piers Caresfoot, your wife has been delivered of a fine girl. But I am bound to tell you that her condition is far from good. It's a most complicated and dangerous case.

He looks more closely at the corpse.

PIERS:

A girl. Why did it have to be a girl? My son would still have inherited according to the new will but now everything except this house goes to Douglas.

DR. SURREY:

How did he go? In pain, I fear.

PIERS:

We were talking together when suddenly he was seized with the attack. I got the medicine as quick as I could but he knocked the glass out of my hand with a jerk of his head. Next second, he was dead.

DR. SURREY:

This new will leaves you very poor, does it not?

PIERS:

I shall manage barely. Two of the outlying farms are mine through my mother's will.

DR. SURREY:

If you ever should need any extra cash, Piers Caresfoot, there is always the sort of work you used to do for me.

PIERS:

Scavenging stray beasts. Oh my God!

He buries his face in his hands.

OWEN:
> At the edge of the forest.

DOUGLAS:
> What's happening at the house?

GERALDINE: *handing him the golden cup*
> This is yours Douglas. You are the new squire of
> Caresfoot Court. The poor cast-off cousin who
> worked in the stables and lurked in the forest and was
> beaten and cuffed by Piers Caresfoot . . . You, you are
> the new squire.

DOUGLAS:
> How did this happen?

GERALDINE:
> The old man's dead and Claudia's baby is a girl.

DOUGLAS:
> How did he die?

GERALDINE:
> Of his heart. Piers was with him.

DOUGLAS:
> That old man was kind to me. I wonder if I've been
> kind to him letting you loose, you hell dog.

GERALDINE:
> I see I get no thanks but where's my payment?

DOUGLAS:
> When can I move into Caresfoot Court and sit in Devil
> Caresfoot's chair?

GERALDINE:

Unfortunately Devil Caresfoot couldn't will you the manorhouse. You'll get it after Piers is dead.

DOUGLAS:

Very well then. You'll get your letters back when I'm the real master of Caresfoot Court. I suppose I must put up at the Grange.

GERALDINE:

Won't you take the cup?

He knocks it out of her hand and gallops off.

GHOST:

Don't you wish, mother dear, that you had yon bonny girl baby that's just been born in your arms?

GERALDINE:

Oh my baby! Cut out my tongue if I don't. I've dug you up from your grave and flung your bones about but still you haunt me. I wish her baby was dead and my baby was alive.

GHOST:

Take my wish bone mother. Here it is by the haunted well. Find it . . . Here . . . There.

Laughing.

Sew up my bone into a doll. Give it to her when she's grown up a bit. And if she loves me and kisses me then I'll have rest for I'll have found my true mother and then I'll not haunt you any more.

GERALDINE:

I'll sew your wishbone into a doll, my bonny child, but I cannot find where I threw it.

GHOST: *laughing*

> Over here mother. Down the crooked path. Here at
> the weasel's den. Here in your crooked heart. Haste
> mother for the dawn comes and then I can speak
> no more.

SCENE 21: DAWN

OWEN:

> The red room at Caresfoot Court. The time . . .
> At dawn.

> *The bed. The crying of a real child. A cock
> crows.*

CLAUDIA:

> My child, you are a messenger sent to call me to a
> happier world. An angel messenger. When I am
> gone see that you call her Angela so I may know
> by what name to call her when the time comes.
> Go quickly, doctor, and tell my husband to come.
> I shall die at dawn.

DR. SURREY:

> Piers, you must come now if you wish to see your
> wife alive.

PIERS:

> Claudia . . .

CLAUDIA:

> Piers, I'm sorry, I could not bear to see you before.
> But I wanted to get all anger at you out of my soul.
> And now I have. Piers, I loved you. Despite all, I
> hope to see you again. My motherless babe, may the
> power of God protect you, angels guard you, and
> may the curse of God fall upon those who would

57

bring evil upon you. Piers, you have heard my words.
In your charge I leave the child. See that you never
betray the trust.

PIERS:

I promise, Claudia. Oh God . . . Why have you cursed
me . . . Death and wickedness, misery and death.

A cock crows.

CLAUDIA:

Piers, give her your love. May God have mercy on
my soul.

*They kneel. Draw the curtains of the bed. Bird
sounds and cockcrow outside, branches against
reddening sky. Look over at the other corpse
on the table. Perhaps also the four giant shadows
of the four genii appear looking down at the
dawn they have made.*

OWEN:

What winds have we been listening to?

CHORUS:

The North Wind. The South Wind.

OWEN:

Then it is time to end Act One.

act two

SCENE 22: BERRY-PICKING

The chorus assemble on the stage. The four listeners drift up the aisles toward the West Room. They are picking berries along the lane.

HARRIET:
    There used to be some wild raspberries along here somewhere.

JENNY:
    There's a bird's nest under the burdock leaves. An oven bird.

    Chorus click two stones together.

JENNY:
    Yes, that's just the sound he makes. Listen!

ANN:
    Do the Jamieson kids always pasture their cows along the side road?

OWEN:

Oh yes, Ann. The roadside grass is free. You might as well use it.

ANN:

And they spend the whole summer just herding the cattle up and down the road.

OWEN:

Yes. Except when they come in to help us with the play.

HARRIET:
A great big spiderweb.

OWEN:

Do you want the berries or don't you?

HARRIET:
No.

OWEN:

Just brush him away like that. He'll build another web somewhere else. Here have the berries.

JENNIE:
Where are we now in the play.

ANN:

I'm now writing the history of Angela's childhood.

HARRIET:
I have to practice my skipping.

She begins to skip.

ANN:

Oh how can you on such a hot day.

They all sit down under the elm tree by the well except HARRIET who skips as the chorus sings.

Green Gravel, Green Gravel, your grass is so green
The fairest young damsel that ever was seen
I'll clothe you in silk, and I'll bathe you in milk
And I'll write down your name with a glass pen and ink.

Dear Eileen, dear Eileen, your true love is dead. He
wrote you a letter . . . To turn round your head . . .

OWEN:
> Angela is the child of Claudia and Piers. She grows up
> at Caresfoot Court.

CHORUS:
> Child of delight! With sunbright hair
> And seablue, seadeep eyes;
> Spirit of bliss, what brings thee here
> Beneath these sullen skies?

JENNY:
> She grows up under the care of her old nurse, Martha.
> Her father has become miserly and eccentric.

OWEN:
> Eccentric, yes.

ANN:
> At twilight after he has finished his farming work he
> goes round the countryside with a cage and catches
> stray dogs, runaway dogs and any loose dogs that fall
> in his way.

JENNY:
> What does he do with them?

ANN:
> He puts them in kennels at the back of the Court and
> starves them.

OWEN:
> Does he keep them?

ANN:

No. Every month a doctor comes with a cart and takes all the poor dogs away. Then Piers gets his money and goes out collecting again.

OWEN:

What an end for an Oxford B.A. somehow or other. Which reminds me. We'd better start training our dogs. What kinds of dogs have we got in Piers Caresfoot's kennels?

To the chorus.

CHORUS:

Bloodhounds, beagles, collie dogs, foxhounds, poodles, bulldogs, dachshunds, greyhounds, and terriers.

JENNY:

Do we have to use them? Why not get some real dogs. My dog could act. You should see him.

OWEN:

It's no use, Jenny. Father says he can't stand a dog licking him in the face and if he's tied to a chair and the dog really does begin to eat him . . . Now . . .

To the chorus.

Let's hear these dogs bark. Bloodhound?

A member of the chorus gives forth and so on all down the line.

Beagle? Collie dog? Are you hungry, foxhound? Have you temper, French poodle? Will you hold Douglas by his throat, bulldog? When Angela gives you freedom will you try to eat her, collie dog? Dachshund? When old Piers is tied to his chair will you bite him to his bones, greyhound? Pekingese?

The actor who does the baby ghost gives a faint little bark.

ANN:

What about Angela's education? Who does she
play with?

JENNY:

Her father's dream is to buy back his father's land
from Douglas. He pays no attention to her. But the
local clergyman, Mr. Gleneden, gives her lessons.

HARRIET:

Isn't there a feeble-minded boy who plays around the
yard a lot?

JENNY:

Yes. His name is Rogue. He is a fine child out of
Douglas and a woman in the village. Douglas beat
Rogue so that he ran away and Martha took him in
over at Caresfoot Court.

HARRIET:

What does Douglas do?

The chorus start establishing wind and hoofbeats.

OWEN:

Douglas hunts in the forest. Sets traps. Runs his
farms. Never smiles. Gallops about on his black horse.
Listen! Hear the hooves of his horse underneath the
river of wind!

SCENE 23: NURSERY

A cradle by the great bed.

OWEN:

Caresfoot Court. The Nursery.

*Chorus can hum and whistle a lullaby in the
background.*

ANGELA: *played by HARRIET*
Who is that riding by so late at night, Martha?

MARTHA: *played by TABBY*
Hush ye, hush ye or the Black Huntsman will get ye.

ANGELA:
Listen to the wind blowing in Caresfoot's Staff.

MARTHA:
Hush ye, Angela, or the Black Huntsman will get you.

ANGELA:
How deep is the well at the foot of the great tree?

MARTHA:
Deep as you must sleep, Miss Angela. Hush ye, hush ye or the Goblin Hunter will get ye.

OWEN:
The doll. Caresfoot Court.

> *The whirl of wheels and the sound of hooves on gravel. ANGELA and MARTHA sit by the fire waiting for their visitor.*

ANGELA:
Whose horses are those coming up the drive, Martha?

MARTHA:
It's Lady Eldred's carriage. Perhaps she's come to call on your father.

LADY ELDRED: *played by GERALDINE*
No Martha, I've come to see Angela here.

> *They curtsey.*

This is Angela's birthday, is it not? I've come with a present for her. A present that I've made.

A box is handed to ANGELA.

A doll for you, my dear.

ANGELA:
> May I open it, Martha? I've never had a doll of my
> own except that antique one we found in the attic.
> And the rats have chewed it.

MARTHA:
> Open it, Miss Angela, and don't forget to thank her
> ladyship.

> *ANGELA takes out a large rag doll.*

LADY ELDRED:
> Aren't you going to hug and kiss your dolly?

ANGELA:
> Thank you, Lady Eldred, no. I don't think I know
> her well enough yet.

LADY ELDRED:
> Bless the child. How sharp she is, Martha. Why
> Martha, how sad it is to see this fine old place in
> such a ruinous decay. Some of the chimneys have
> toppled and the drive is tangled with weeds and
> underbrush.

MARTHA:
> Mr. Caresfoot has no time to take care of his house,
> m'am.

LADY ELDRED:
> I suppose. Too busy driving cattle, collecting live
> animals and dead ones I hear. Goodbye, Angela.

> *She exits.*

ANGELA:
> Thank you for the doll, Lady Eldred. What do you
> think of my doll, Martha?

MARTHA:
>Here's your porridge, Miss Angela. Oh it's alright as dolls go but I'd throw it in the fire just the same.

>*Over at the table.*

ANGELA:
>Yes, I do hate it. I hate it.

MARTHA:
>There there, darling. What is the matter?

ANGELA:
>I'll just run upstairs and lay the doll on my bed. It makes me feel so strange looking at me. Hark! Listen, Martha.

MARTHA:
>It's Master Douglas galloping away on his black horse. He's been to see your father.

PIERS:
>Angela, Cousin Douglas has been telling me that someone from Caresfoot Court interferes with his traps.

ANGELA:
>I interfere, father. I spring open everyone I can find.

PIERS:
>Angela, some day I intend to ask Douglas if he will let me buy back Caresfoot from him. We must humour him.

ANGELA:
>Father, I'm not going to walk to school with rabbits and other poor things twisting their hearts out by my feet.

PIERS:

> Don't look at me like that, Angela.

He turns sharply away.

SCENE 24: TRAPS

OWEN:

> The vicarage.

> *ANGELA walks over to the vicarage on stage*
> *left to be tutored by MR. GLENEDEN, the Vicar.*
> *He could be played by the same actor as played*
> *Devil Caresfoot, but without beard.*

GLENEDEN:

> Good afternoon, Angela. What are you going to recite
> for me today?

> *She recites a La Fontaine Fable, mouthing*
> *it under the next scene. Over by the well,*
> *DOUGLAS and ROGUE enter, setting traps. The*
> *chorus can provide slapping sounds for the trap*
> *sounds, but too, they are to be a flock of birds in*
> *a thicket. When DOUGLAS fires at them with a*
> *cap pistol, they must fly away to just under the*
> *front of the stage where they pretend to be dogs*
> *in the Caresfoot kennels.*

DOUGLAS:

> Come Rogue. Spring this trap open and I'll put the
> bait in.

ROGUE:

> Oh I'm afraid of these traps, mister.

DOUGLAS:

> What're you afraid of? It doesn't hurt me.

He catches his hand in a trap.

DOUGLAS:
Come on, try it.

ROGUE: *screaming*
Alright, mister.

DOUGLAS:
Well, you poor idiot, how else are you going to get your hands as tough as mine.

He unsprings him.

Now they're all set. Three in the copse and two in the hazel thicket, one at the roots of Caresfoot's Staff, one at the culvert, and Rogue I'll set you to watch out for the girl who thinks she can spring any trap of mine. Rogue, look here, this thicket is alive with young partridges. Let's see if I can pick off a few.

Cap pistol. DOUGLAS laughs as the birds fly off. The chorus goes offstage to get into the kennels in front of the stage. ANGELA is heard again over at the vicarage.

ANGELA:
Mr. Gleneden, what lies over there behind those hills. Beyond the forest. Is it the sea?

GLENEDEN:
No, Angela. It isn't the sea.

ANGELA:
Father will never let me walk beyond our fences, but sometimes when I'm gathering wood in the forest with Martha, I think I hear voices on the other side of the wall in some other house.

GLENEDEN:
You've probably strayed near Hawskcliffe Hall. There is a boy there your age.

ANGELA:
Why doesn't he come over and play with Rogue and me?

GLENEDEN:
My dear girl, your father quarrelled with the lady at Hawkscliffe Hall a long time ago and they have not spoken since.

ANGELA:
I wonder what about?

GLENEDEN:
Run along now, Angela or Martha will say I make you late for your tea.

On the way home ANGELA takes a willow switch and springs the traps.

ANGELA:
Three in the copse. Two in the hazel thicket. One at the roots of Caresfoot's Staff. Why Rogue, whatever have you done to your hand?

ROGUE:
Father made me put my hand in a trap.

ANGELA:
Just a moment and I'll bandage up your hand. Why this trap by the culvert has caught something already. Look, Rogue, a little white puppy. Aw, is your paw badly hurt. Here, I'll bind up both your paws together.

She tears a handkerchief in half.

I wonder whose puppy this is?

ARTHUR: *played by OWEN*
He's mine. He ran away on me this morning and I've been looking for him all the day.

ANGELA:
>Well he had his paw in one of our traps but he's alright now. Let's put him in this basket so he can nurse his paw. Now you can play with us.

ARTHUR:
>What do you play?

ANGELA:
>Anything you like.

ARTHUR:
>That's a monstrous deep well you got here.

>>*He hollers down it.*

ANGELA:
>It's a haunted well. Rogue and I have a game we play with it.

>>*She and ROGUE place a plank across the well on the chairs and walk back and forth across it. ARTHUR joins them.*

>Now we have another game. Can you lift your own weight, boy?

>>*Play this at the trap door.*

ARTHUR:
>My name's Arthur. Sure I can.

ANGELA:
>Well, we hang ourselves down the well like this and then pull ourselves up again.

>>*Mime this with the trap door.*

ARTHUR:
>Help! I can't get up.

>>*ANGELA and ROGUE pull him out.*

ROGUE:

> You aren't as strong as I am.

ARTHUR:

> Oh yes I am. I can throw you.

> *He wrestles and throws ROGUE.*

ANGELA:

> Shame on you for hurting a poor boy who's not right in the head.

> *She stamps her foot as Claudia did earlier.*

ARTHUR:

> I can throw you too.

> *ANGELA puts a cushion on the ground.*

> What are you putting that on the ground for?

ANGELA:

> Because you're going to need it when you hit the ground.

> *They wrestle and ANGELA throws him down. He gets up in a rage.*

ARTHUR:

> I'll never come here to play again. I hate you.

ANGELA:

> I'm sorry, are you terribly hurt? I thought the cushion would break your fall. I really did, I really did . . . Ah, come on, Arthur. Why don't you come and see my father's kennels. We've got all the stray dogs for miles around.

ARTHUR:

> Then this is the place my mother warned me about. And I see now what you were going to do with my

puppy. Your father collects dogs and steals them and
starves them and sells them to Doctor Surrey for
vivisection at his surgical school. Mother says it's the
most contemptible way of making money she's ever
heard.

ANGELA:

That's not true. Get off the property. I never want to
see you again. Oh Martha, it's not true what he says.

ARTHUR:

You don't even know what vivisection means, do you?
It means cutting up alive. And they say in the village
when little kids are naughty, watch out or old Mr.
Caresfoot will get you. So there.

He exits.

MARTHA:

Pay no heed to him, Miss Angela.

ANGELA:

Oh I see it all now. He and Douglas work together.
The latter takes the fur and father feeds the carcasses
to the dogs only there's never enough to go around.
But it all costs nothing. I'm going to let them go.
Hands off me.

Start dog barking here by chorus.

If I hear one more trap click and one more knife
whetted and one more animal barking at dawn . . .

*She dashes at the kennels and lets the dogs go.
PIERS comes in with a whip.*

PIERS:

Who the devil told her to do that. Those dogs are so
hungry they'll eat her alive. Get down! Get away!
Draw them off, Martha. They've got her down!

He whips at the dogs.

MARTHA:
Help, master. They're eating Miss Angela alive!

> *DOUGLAS enters with a gun and shoots the principal hound. PIERS picks up ANGELA and puts her on the bed.*

SCENE 25: SICKBED

> *ANGELA sick in bed, tended by MARTHA. JENNY announces this.*

MARTHA:
This is the third day of your fever, Miss Angela.

ANGELA:
Could you comb my hair, Martha. That's not my comb.

> *LADY ELDRED stands in the shadows and makes a sinister delirium sound with a button that spins on a string.*

MARTHA:
You've lost your comb, Miss Angela. The night of the storm you were walking in your sleep. You must have lost your comb somewhere in the forest.

ANGELA:
Poor comb. Mother's comb. It has a golden star in its ivory shaft. I wonder how long it will lie in the wind and the rain before the ravens find it.

MARTHA:
How do you feel now, Miss Angela?

ANGELA:
> Why Martha, I can see you quite clearly. Was I feverish?

MARTHA:
> You made me hide Lady Eldred's doll. You said it was crawling up the covers at you.

ANGELA:
> So it was. It looks at me. I used to think I could stand it but I guess I can't Martha!

MARTHA:
> Yes, miss.

ANGELA:
> Martha, I had the dream about the slaughter house again. Do you remember when we walked into the village and I climbed up over the fence? There was a great pool of blood on the ground. And then it began to snow. And the snow fell into the pool of blood. Do you remember?

MARTHA:
> Yes, Miss Angela.

ANGELA:
> Do you hear a humming sound?

MARTHA:
> No, Miss Angela.

ANGELA:
> Could I look out the window, Martha?

> *The nurse helps her to the window.*

The moon is struggling with the clouds. But the night wind soon will clear them from her face.

> *The curtains billow out around them.*

A horseman gallops by.

Martha, do you remember when I was very little I used to ask who that was riding by at night?

MARTHA:
Hush ye, hush ye or the Black Huntsman will get ye.

ANGELA:
Someday, Martha, I see that I may have to ride with him. But not very far. Only to the star that shines on my mother's lost comb.

SCENE 26: VERANDAH

ANGELA rises. MARTHA prepares MRS. TAYLOR's tray of food. OWEN's father comes in and sits on a chair on the verandah dozing in the summer heat. HARRIET and OWEN's mother walk up and down as if it were the verandah of the farmhouse. HARRIET throws up maple keys from a brown paper bag she is carrying. They helicopter down above their heads.

MOTHER:
Harriet, you said you had something to say to me. Out with it, my girl.

HARRIET:
Alright, aunt. I'm not afraid. Get mad if you like but we think that you should come back and live with your husband.

MOTHER: *growling*
Who's we?

HARRIET:
>Me . . . And Jenny and Ann.

MOTHER:
>Why should I?

HARRIET:
>Because it's breaking Owen's heart.

MOTHER:
>Tabby, hurry up with that tray. I'm famished.

TABBY:
>Yes, Mrs. Taylor. I've got your sandwiches made but your tea hasn't steeped yet.

MOTHER:
>Bring me the whole pot. I'll steep it myself.

HARRIET:
>Perhaps I could bring your tea out to you, aunt.

MOTHER:
>Don't bother being thoughtful, Harriet. It's just a waste of time. So I should go back with my husband, eh? I suppose you think your father and mother should get together again, eh?

HARRIET:
>Yes. And I know they will.

>>*TABBY brings the tray. Mother inspects the sandwiches.*

MOTHER:
>That lettuce looks very much like burdock to me, Tabby.

TABBY:
>Good for your blood, Mrs. Taylor.

MOTHER: *giving her one sandwich*
Here put that one back in the incubator. It doesn't
look like lettuce to me.

> *She samples the tea right from the teapot's spout
> as TABBY retreats.*

Well see here, niece Harriet. I don't care about Owen.
I don't care about my husband. I care a bit about my
horses.

FATHER:
My horses, you mean.

MOTHER:
I don't care about myself. In the fall I'm going away
with a friend and by that time Owen'll be dead. If
he isn't he'll never see me again.

HARRIET:
How can you be cruel like that?

MOTHER:
You don't understand, Harriet.

HARRIET: *running off*
No, I'm glad I don't either.

FATHER:
What was Harriet asking you to do, my dear one?

MOTHER:
She has the childish idea that we should get together
again.

FATHER:
It's an idea I suppose.

MOTHER:
Just look at you sitting there with that silly little grin
and the curls. Too weak to raise your arm. Well, raise
your arm. Ah, you see, you can't even raise your arm.

FATHER:

Everything was placid till you and Harriet started arguing on the verandah. Why did you come back anyhow?

MOTHER:

To say goodbye to Owen. To be at his play. In it too.

FATHER:

You're really after my other good horse, aren't you?

MOTHER:

Perhaps. You're too feckless to stop me. You know it's almost as if you drank but it isn't drink that makes you so stupid . . . It's air. Just the air you breathe. And inside, you're rotten. The baby girl you gave me died. Now the baby boy is. I want nothing more to do with you.

FATHER:

I know. Our whole case is in Darwin. The sixth volume of Coral Reefs. The family that all either dies at seventeen or lived to seventy-five. Generation after generation. I had what Owen has but I got over it.

MOTHER: *going out stage left*
Yes, yes.

FATHER:

Wait a minute. Owen wants us now. Come back and eat your lunch with us if you must.

The chorus start coming up on stage for the next scene.

MOTHER:
Oh very well.

She makes a hurried lunch, wiping off her mouth as the next scene begins where she must play the hostess.

78

OWEN: *himself about to play ARTHUR*
An afternoon party at the Eldred's.

LADY ELDRED: *played by MRS. TAYLOR who is*
speaking to ANGELA and PIERS as they enter.
Ah, how do you do, Mr. Caresfoot. It is some time
since we met.

PIERS:
Angela, let me introduce you to Lady Eldred and
Sir Eldred.

LADY ELDRED:
You are even handsomer than your mother and she
always killed me if I were in the same room with her.

ANGELA:
Thank you, Lady Eldred.

LADY ELDRED:
Pray let me introduce you to Mr. Arthur Brenzaida.
Mr. Brenzaida is over at Hawkscliffe you know but he
has been away for years in Madeira. Miss Angela
Caresfoot, Mr. Arthur Brenzaida.

ANGELA:
What were you doing in Madeira, Mr. Brenzaida?

ARTHUR:
Father had a plantation there, Miss Caresfoot. Mother
and I managed it after his death and then when she
died I came north again to Hawkscliffe. I have been
selling some land to your cousin Douglas.

ANGELA:
And then what will you do?

ARTHUR:
I shall travel for a year and then study for the bar.

ANGELA:
> Is Madeira a sunny island with green palm trees off the coast of Africa?

ARTHUR:
> Yes. You're the first young lady I've met who's known where it is. Someone must have taught you your geography awfully well. Is there anything the matter, Miss Caresfoot?

ANGELA:
> No. It's just that I'm so happy. Do you know that this is the first party I've ever been to. Father had me go to a dressmaker to get my first party dress made and I see we're going to be served more food than I've seen in my whole life. My first party, Mr. Brenzaida!

> *DOUGLAS looks in at a window the prop girl holds up.*

LADY ELDRED:
> Your daughter seems to have acquired a lover already, Mr. Caresfoot. What a pleasant surprise that it should be Maria's boy. Ah, Douglas. We have all been like sheep without a shepherd though I saw you keeping an eye on the flock through the window.

DOUGLAS:
> I wanted to see who was here. Her! Who is she?

LADY ELDRED:
> Why Douglas, she's the little girl who used to spring all your traps. Angela Caresfoot.

SIR EDWARD:
> Congratulations, my dear Mr. Brenzaida. I am told that this morning your dog Keeper killed that savage beast Douglas Caresfoot has about. Bit me in the fat of my leg last autumn when I was over shooting.

ARTHUR:

>I'm afraid that my dog and I aren't too popular down at Douglas's place right now.

PIERS:

>Angela, I would like you to pay attention to Douglas. He is very fond of pretty women and between us we might beguile him into selling me back my land.

ANGELA.

>Father, I do not in the least understand you.

PIERS:

>How often Angela have I asked you not to stare me out of countenance. It is a most unladylike trick of yours.

ANGELA:

>I beg your pardon. I forgot. I will look out the window.

PIERS:

>Look sometimes at Douglas. Let me have something. I bought you that dress. Angela, you don't understand. Once I was a gentleman. Now I'm a cattle drover and deal in dead animals. I want to be a gentleman again before I die and I'm saving up the money that I have to have. But the money's no use unless my land comes back with it. Angela, I lost Caresfoot because I married your mother and you were a girl!

>*She walks away from him.*

ARTHUR:

>I have something for you.

>*He gives her the comb.*

ANGELA:

>My mother's comb. Why Mr. Brenzaida, I lost this comb years ago when I was a child.

ARTHUR:

I found it this morning in the forest near your place. The rain last night washed away the dead leaves that covered it.

ANGELA:

Aren't you the boy who came over to play and we . . . Your white puppy got caught in one of our traps . . . We hung down the sides of the well. And then I . . . Oh we fought like wild cats.

ARTHUR:

Of course! Why of course!

ANGELA: .

I brought out a cushion and I flung you down.

They laugh together.

DOUGLAS:

Take me over to her Geraldine. She's the girl I mean to marry and you shall manage it for me.

LADY ELDRED leads DOUGLAS to ANGELA and ARTHUR. It is a hypnotic moment. Just as he is about to reach out for ANGELA's hand, he trips over a footstool and falls flat at her feet. ANGELA and ARTHUR run away laughing. As they run off, they throw maple keys at everybody.

SCENE 28: THE NIGHT WIND

OWEN lies down on the bed. HARRIET enters.

FATHER: *off*

Ten o'clock, Owen. Time to light up your night light, stop reading and compose yourself for slumber.

MARTHA:
>You need all the sleep you can get Owen with all the people coming tomorrow and the play and everything.

OWEN:
>O.k. Couldn't Harriet stay up a bit and talk to me? Sit down, Harriet.

HARRIET:
>How are you, Owen?

OWEN:
>I'm fine. You don't have to talk. I just like to lie here and listen to the night winds.

HARRIET:
>The crickets have just started.

>*Chorus can make cricket noises with combs.*

>It's surprising how soon everything's ripe. The dandelions are hardly up before they're greyheaded.

OWEN:
>Yes. Harriet, did you have any luck with mother today?

HARRIET:
>Not really. She just got mad and talked so oddly to your father.

OWEN:
>But we introduced the subject. I'll put it to her after the play.

HARRIET:
>Owen, I'd give the whole world if she'd stay tho' I don't really like her . . . And if you'd get better . . .

OWEN:
>Why?

HARRIET:

Isn't it funny . . . Because I've always felt or used to feel when I was quite small that when we grew up we'd get married.

OWEN:

Aren't we first cousins? Mother and Tabby used to always beat the drum against first cousin marriages. And given my hereditary disease . . . Still, if I get better this summer . . . It's an idea, isn't it?

HARRIET:

Yes. That's all it is, Owen. An idea.

The cricket sounds, then the night wind sounds.

SCENE 29: THE NIGHT WIND SPEAKS

OWEN: *rising*

The Night Wind.

CHORUS:

First the North Wind, the South Wind, now the Night Wind.

OWEN:

Four chairs can be anything. They can be the pig-keeper's hut by a stream in the forest whose leaves are beloved by the night wind.

CHORUS:

The Night Wind

Have we not been from childhood friends?
Have I not loved thee long?
As long as thou hast loved the night
Whose silence wakes my song.

84

SCENE 30: A SECOND HUT IN THE FOREST

ARTHUR:
>Look Angela, someone has carved their initials on the rough plank here.

ANGELA:
>D.C. and G.A. Douglas Caresfoot and Geraldine . . . Her maiden name was Almeda. Yes. When they were very young Martha says they were in love.

ARTHUR:
>Look! Here's a battered old tin box hidden up above the door. Look!

ANGELA:
>Some ribbons and a paste diamond brooch. Poor thing, she made herself beautiful for him.

ARTHUR:
>Some old candles.

ANGELA:
>Oh Arthur. Let's light them and fasten them to chips of wood and see how long they'll float down the stream.

ARTHUR: *lighting candles*
>Where does this stream come from Angela?

>*The chorus unfolds and waves a long strip of gauze which comes from the stage and up an aisle. ARTHUR and ANGELA play beside it.*

ANGELA:
>From the haunted well at the foot of Caresfoot's Staff. This one's Arthur. This one's Angela.

>*They chase after the candle boats which drawn by strings dart down the stream across and off the stage, reappearing on the other side.*

SCENE 31: AT THE GRANGE

> *DOUGLAS and GERALDINE now occupy the stage.*

JENNY:
The Grange.

DOUGLAS: *lounging while she stands*
Now listen to this one Geraldine. I wonder who it was wrote this dainty note? Dear Douglas, last night I experimented with our brat. I tried my hand at choking it but found it harder to choke a whelp than you might at first suppose.

GERALDINE:
I wrote that. Why do you torture me about something that can't be undone?

DOUGLAS:
I torture you because you have to be tortured back into shape. You're getting to be such a fine lady. Of course you're not a fine lady at all, you're my right hand. Geraldine, the day I marry Angela Caresfoot . . . On that day I will burn these uncomfortable letters before your eyes. And Sir Edward will never see them.

GERALDINE:
Douglas! Have some pity. Don't drive me to destroy such a pretty young girl.

DOUGLAS:
It's laughable to hear you pitying your successful rival.

GERALDINE:
I . . . Pity her? I hate her. Look you, I suffer. She shall suffer more. Her love will be fouled and her life made a shambles. Such a shambles that she will cease to believe there is a God. In return I shall give her . . . *You.*

DOUGLAS: *clapping*
>Bravo! But don't just stand there. You're going to
>have to work harder than that for your letters
>Geraldine. It's through her father Piers Caresfoot
>that we must work first. And I need some money
>to work him. Here's my cheque book. Now go away.
>I want to walk up and down in this room in the
>firelight.

>>*The lovers pursue the candles across the stage
>>again until the stream widens and they come
>>across a boat.*

ANGELA:
>Here's an old boat, Arthur. Take off your shoes and
>we'll pole it down into the lake.

>>*With poles they mime going down a stream.
>>Sometimes the current spins them around. They
>>arrive at an island in the lake.*

ARTHUR:
>My candle's still going, Angela.

ANGELA:
>Oh Arthur, my candle's drowned. But the moon shall
>be my candle and she is brighter now than the day.

SCENE 32: SHALL SHE DIE?

>>*The four children stand by the four chairs and
>>put straws in a Bible.*

ALL:
>Shall she live or shall she die? Owen, one of the straws
>is shorter than all the others. You draw for Angela.

OWEN:

Poor lovely. See? She dies. We'll end the play with
her death.

ANN:

Owen, you always like killing them off and then I have
to write up the death scene.

JENNY:

Doesn't it sometimes frighten you . . . How much we
know about Caresfoot Court and no one else does.

OWEN:

Last night I dreamt I was at Caresfoot Court. I was
Arthur . . . I'd got locked in the yards at the back
where the dogs are kept and I couldn't get out. I woke
up thinking why couldn't I have been a normal person
instead of always dreaming it out. Always listening to
the wind.

ANN:

I worship the world we make up stories about. I can
never stop thinking about new things for Geraldine to
say and do. It's idolatry . . . And yet I can't live
without it . . . Without dreaming it out.

HARRIET:

I don't feel guilty. The wind we listen to blows white
sails to . . .

SCENE 33: ETERNITY CHORUS

CHORUS:

Eternity

I sat in silent musing,
The soft wind waved my hair,
"O come," it sighed so sweetly,
"I'll win thee 'gainst thy will."

"Have we not been from childhood friends?
  Have I not loved thee long?
  As long as thou hast loved the night
  Whose silence wakes my song."

"And when thy heart is laid at rest
  Beneath the churchyard stone
  I shall have time enough to mourn
  And thou to be alone . . ."

The Night Wind   The Night Wind   The Night Wind

SCENE 34: CHURCH BELLS

PIERS:

Ah Brenzaida, you're back from church. Never mind looking about for Angela. What I want to say concerns her though.

ARTHUR:

Sir, this provides me with an opportunity to ask you something first. May Angela and I become engaged?

PIERS:

Ah yes . . . But on one condition. That is what I want to speak to you about. You may become engaged if you do not see each other or to communicate with one another by letters for one whole year . . . Beginning today.

ARTHUR:

Mr. Caresfoot, you quite take my breath away. If you say we can be engaged why must we not see each other for a whole year?

PIERS:

Oh Mr. Brenzaida, it's a test to see if you really do love Angela and if Angela really loves you.

ARTHUR:
Otherwise?

PIERS:
I forbid your engagement entirely.

ARTHUR:
Yours are hard terms.

PIERS:
But they are my terms. Angela . . . You have been listening. Your father proposes to test your youthful ecstasy.

ANGELA:
You will not forget me in a year, will you Arthur?

He kisses her.

PIERS:
Don't look at me like that, Angela.

ANGELA:
But father. These are cruel terms . . . To be dead to each other for a whole long year.

PIERS:
I cannot help it. I'm looking at your real happiness. Why don't you visit your father's plantation in Madeira, Mr. Brenzaida? If you agree to my conditions you should leave by the four o'clock train. Come, I've been kind enough today.

ANGELA:
I am your daughter and should obey you. Surely you wish to do what is best for me. Even though I will be wretched for a year, I accept. Arthur, I'd say no except it's the first time really that my father has shown himself caring what I did.

ARTHUR:

Mr. Caresfoot, if Angela agrees then I agree. You've cornered us. But you won't make me forget Angela. Nor will she me. So unless one of us dies before the year is up I shall come back to be married to Angela on the ninth of June.

PIERS:

Don't forget to bring at that date, Mr. Brenzaida, a marriage settlement of say, half your property on Angela.

ARTHUR:

On those terms I give you my promise.

PIERS:

Very good, then that is settled. I'll send for a cart to take you to the train.

ANGELA:

Father, Arthur and I can walk to the station. It will be our last walk together for many a day. Arthur, wait for me till I get my bonnet.

PIERS sits in his chair as if transfixed by some vision. Walking into the village the lovers should cross over a bridge, a plank over two chairs.

ARTHUR:

Angela, such a funny thing with your father. When I dropped in again to say goodbye he was sitting in his chair staring at some shadows on the wall outside his window. He didn't move. He couldn't even see me.

ANGELA:

I know, I've seen him in that state. Father has ghosts in his life, you know. Why when this fit is on him Martha once said you could tie him to his chair and he'd not know.

Keeper barks. They restrain him.

ANGELA:
> There's the slaughterhouse, Arthur. That's the dog
> that guards it. And the lane into Douglas's house.
> Ah, what a dark green shadowy tunnel that is for the
> black stallion to come shooting out of.

ARTHUR:
> Do you hear music?

ANGELA:
> I've been hearing it for sometime. Look Arthur, it's
> an old beggar fiddling under the trees at the edge of
> the common.

> *Towards them, as if they are walking towards*
> *him, comes a disreputable but vaguely gentle-*
> *manly-looking violinist. They put some money*
> *in his case and dance to his music. When the*
> *piece is finished, he slouches off.*

ARTHUR:
> He's going into the tavern to spend the money I
> gave him.

ANGELA:
> Poor fellow. Arthur, what about your dog Keeper?
> I shall miss you Keeper almost as much as your
> master.

ARTHUR:

You'll not miss him Angela because I'm going to
make you a present of him . . . If you'll accept him.
Go to Angela, Keeper!

ANGELA:

Why Keeper! Did you hear that? You're my dog
now. Arthur, hold out your hand. There take my
ring.

ARTHUR:

What a beautiful crest. Has it always been yours?

ANGELA:

In my mother's family it has been a very old ring.
That is the star of love in the deep blue of the evening
sky.

ARTHUR:

What does the strange writing say underneath?

ANGELA:

It means "forever". Be true to me, Arthur. Keep the
ring and give it back to me when we meet again.

ARTHUR:

I promise, Angela. My life, my love!

*The train takes him away. Use the crossbuck or
sighnpost used in the earlier station scene.*

SCENE 35: OH, MR. GLENEDEN

*ANGELA stands a long time waving after the
train, then whirls about and walks across through
the chorus (forest) to the vicarage, where several
months later she is now speaking to MR.
GLENEDEN.*

CHORUS:

The East Wind

All hushed and still within the house;
Without — all wind and driving rain;
But something whispers to my mind,
Through rain and through the wailing wind . . .

The wind that comes from across the sea!
The fierce howling mother and the rain, her doll!
Sss Sss Sssss Ssss Sssss

JENNY:

The vicarage.

ANGELA:

Mr. Gleneden, you are my minister and old teacher.
Could I talk to you for a while?

GLENEDEN:

Angela, your hands are cold with the East Wind that
blows so bitterly today. My favourite old scholar,
what can possibly ail a healthy and pretty young
woman such as you are?

ANGELA:

First of all, Mr. Gleneden, you must understand that
I'm engaged.

GLENEDEN:

Ah! I had not heard of that.

ANGELA:

And father has sent my fiance, Arthur Brenzaida, out
of the country for a year to test our love. But the
moment Arthur left they began to persecute me.

GLENEDEN:

Who began to persecute you?

ANGELA:

Father, Lady Eldred, my cousin, Douglas.

*ANGELA walks over to have the scene with
DOUGLAS at the well.*

DOUGLAS:
Cousin Angela, so I have found you out at last. What,
are you not going to shake hands with me?

ANGELA:
My father's not at home.

DOUGLAS:
I didn't come to see your father. I came to see you
of whom I can never see enough.

ANGELA:
I wish you'd say something I can understand.

Keeper growls.

DOUGLAS:
If you wish me to sit down you must call that brute
away.

ANGELA:
Keeper is not a brute.

DOUGLAS:
By the way, Angela, I am happy to see that you have
got over your flirtation with young Arthur. Angela,
I might as well tell you he was only flirting and
playing the fool with you.

*ANGELA walks to centre stage for the next
scene with her father.*

PIERS:
Angela, you don't need me to protect you from
Douglas. After all what does he want?

ANGELA:
To marry me I suppose.

PIERS:

Well that's not persecuting you. If you could get young Brenzaida out of your head you might do far worse than marry Douglas.

ANGELA:

Don't talk to me like that. And then . . .

Going back to ELDRED and turning.

In November, when the stream that runs through the forest was raving with the flood of cold rain which the East Wind had brought and still is bringing on the bridge I met Lady Eldred and she said to me.

Chorus members set up a plank bridge between two chairs. GERALDINE and ANGELA approach this from opposite sides of the stage and climb up on the planks. Two chorus members wave the gauze stream under the bridge.

GERALDINE:

Am I to tell your cousin Douglas that you will have nothing to do with him?

ANGELA:

Yes. Even if I were not engaged to Arthur I would not marry Douglas. I've always been afraid of him.

GERALDINE:

Ah! Angela, I find it amusing to hear you talk so and then to think that within seven months you will certainly be Mrs. Douglas Caresfoot.

ANGELA:

Never! What makes you say such horrible things?

GERALDINE:

Because I reflect that Douglas Caresfoot had made up his mind to marry you and I have made up mine to help him to do so and that your will, strong as it certainly is, is as compared with our united wills

what a dead leaf is to this strong East Wind. Angela,
the leaf cannot travel against the wind. It *must* go
with it and you *must* marry Douglas Caresfoot.
You will as certainly come to the altar rails with him
as you will to your deathbed. It is written in your
face. Goodbye, Angela.

> *They return to their respective sides of the stage.*
> *ANGELA continues with GLENEDEN. DOUGLAS*
> *steps forward to read his letter. GERALDINE*
> *prompts him.*

ANGELA:
    Some months ago Sir Edward and Lady Eldred went
    abroad somewhere to the South . . . Sir Edward's
    lungs are bad. Then I received this letter from
    Douglas.

DOUGLAS:
    Loveliest and wildest of creatures. My dear dear
    cousin. I write to say that I accept your verdict
    and that you need fear no further advances from
    me. I know I shall die without you but all the same
    I wish you happiness in the path you now have taken.
    Your affectionate cousin, Douglas Caresfoot.

GLENEDEN:
    Then what have you to be afraid of, Angela?

ANGELA:
    Mr. Gleneden, I feel that they're not through with
    me yet. Some evening I'll hear the hooves of horses
    and the wheels making a hollow sound as they come up
    over the bridge. I'll know then that she's back in
    England with something for me.

SCENE 36: A DISCUSSION

Suddenly the four children are talking, seated or
standing around the four chairs.

HARRIET:

If your mother is really coming back, Owen, is she
sleeping in your father's room or what?

ANN:

Yes, where is she sleeping?

OWEN: *warily*

Oh she's sleeping where mothers usually sleep.

JENNY:

There are five bedrooms in this house. Ann and
Harriet in one, me and Martha in one. My goodness,
does that woman ever snore. Your father. You're
down here, Owen. She could be simply turning in on
a mattress or something in the spare room.

OWEN:

She's with father. She stayed in his room. Tabby
told me.

ANN:

Of course I used to think that meant something.
But from what I've been reading lately you can sleep
in the same room with your husband or your wife and
hate them cold as stone.

OWEN:

I don't see how that could be.

JENNY:

How are we going to suggest this tropical island where
Arthur waits out his year.

ANN:

I think that Caruso record. That sounds very southern.

OWEN:

> And that potted palm from the parlour. And also
> let's hear your sea sounds.

SCENE 37: THE SEA

> *The chorus make sea sounds.*

OWEN:

> No, that's the Mediterranean. Madeira is in the
> Atlantic.

>> *The chorus set up the potted palm and make
>> louder sea sounds.*

> No, no. This is the Atlantic near the equator.

>> *The chorus adjust their sea sounds. They also
>> mime a gramaphone. Someone sings a few bars
>> of Italian à la Caruso.*

CHORUS:

> And then I thought of Ula's bower
> Beyond the southern sea;
> Her tropic prairies bright with flowers
> And rivers wandering free.

SCENE 38: MADEIRA

JENNY:

> Madeira.

>> *A luncheon scene in Madeira with the ELDREDS,
>> JULIA, a young English widow, and ARTHUR.
>> They fan themselves to suggest tropical heat.
>> There is perhaps a servant.*

JULIA:

>Lady Eldred, I believe you know the girl back in England to whom Mr. Brenzaida is engaged.

LADY ELDRED:

>Ah yes, I know her well.

JULIA:

>I am quite curious to hear what she is like.

LADY ELDRED:

>As to her person, Angela Caresfoot is one of the most beautiful women I have ever seen. As to her character, she is deep as the haunted well at her father's house and is as filled with strange springy fantasies and musings combined with a simple forgiving innocence. A woman, I might add, immeasurably above the man on whom she has set her affections.

JULIA:

>That cannot be.

LADY ELDRED:

>Ah but it is. Let me tell you what you are thinking, Mrs. Elbe. That Angela is a formidable rival for his love?

JULIA:

>Yes, something like that.

LADY ELDRED:

>I have been a sort of widow too in my day and know your situation. I may and I may not be of some assistance to you.

>>*ARTHUR and SIR EDWARD come down the verandah to the ladies.*

ARTHUR:

>Sir Edward tells me that you sail for England tomorrow, Lady Eldred.

LADY ELDRED:
>Yes, Sir Edward's bronchitis has been immeasurably bettered by our trip to the Cape.

ARTHUR:
>Will you do something for me?

LADY ELDRED:
>What is that, Mr. Brenzaida?

ARTHUR:
>Tell Angela all about me.

LADY ELDRED:
>Didn't you promise not to communicate with Angela for a year, Mr. Brenzaida?

ARTHUR:
>I know but you didn't.

LADY ELDRED:
>Very well. I shall tell Angela I saw you and perhaps more if her father gives permission. What ring is that you wear?

ARTHUR:
>It's Angela's ring. She gave it to me.

LADY ELDRED:
>May I see it, Mr. Brenzaida?

ARTHUR:
>Very well.

>*He takes off the ring and shows it to her.*

LADY ELDRED:
>Ah. What a pretty ring. The evening star in an azure sky. What does the inscription mean?

ARTHUR:
>"Forever."

LADY ELDRED:

Isn't that better for a wedding ring?

ARTHUR:

Why?

LADY ELDRED:

Because engagements are like the promises and pie crust, made to be broken.

ARTHUR:

That shall not be the case with our engagement.

LADY ELDRED:

Very well, Mr. Brenzaida. Sir Edward and I, when we return to England, we will be sure to give this ring to Angela Caresfoot.

ARTHUR:

I beg your pardon Lady Eldred, but I don't want you to give it to Angela. Give it here.

He puts the ring back on again.

LADY ELDRED:

Would not this ring mean more to her than a thousand descriptions of you from myself? Her ring warm from your finger?

ARTHUR:

Yes. You're right I suppose. Here take the ring to Angela. I myself had hoped to give it to her but tell her that I could not wait so long so sent it ahead with you Lady Eldred.

CHORUS:

The East Wind   The East Wind   The East Wind

SCENE 39: THE GRANGE

JENNY:
>The Grange.

>>*DOUGLAS lounges. SIR EDWARD holds up a long mirror as LADY ELDRED helps ROGUE dress up in one of ARTHUR's suits. ROGUE struts about, highly pleased.*

ROGUE:
>Aye. It is wonderful how fine clothes make you feel fine. Why I look in the glass and I think it's Mister Arthur there only I can't get through to him.

SIR EDWARD:
>The resemblance to Arthur Brenzaida certainly is uncanny once we got him cleaned up and polished. Douglas, I had no idea you and Maria Lawry ever got together.

DOUGLAS:
>That cornstarch pudding. I'd as soon have touched that whey faced bluestocking as I'd make love to a spotted cow. No, the resemblance can't be explained that way Edward. Brenzaida had a younger sister. I came across her in the forest one day and got that for my pains. Nine months later.

SIR EDWARD:
>Rogue is Arthur's first cousin then.

DOUGLAS:
>Of a sort.

ROGUE:
>Do you really think Miss Angela will mistake me for Arthur and give me a kiss?

LADY ELDRED:
>Give you a kiss. She'll embrace you in a frenzy. We'll knock on the door and say, Angela, guess who's come back from the sunny south to his little English snowflake. Drink this glass of wine, Rogue. It will give you gentlemanly confidence.

ROGUE: *sputtering*
>What's this pail of mud doing here on the table?

>>*LADY ELDRED puts her hands in it and watches him.*

LADY ELDRED:
>It's mud to put on your silly doltish face so that when you lie in your coffin Miss Angela will look in and dread to kiss the slubbery decay of tropical death from her fair Arthur's face.

>>*She slathers ROGUE's face with mud as he collapses in EDWARD's arms.*

>There the drug I have put in his wine will keep him deathly still for a night but if we bury him tonight we must dig him up before dawn. Well why are you all looking at me like that?

>>*They put him in the coffin.*

DOUGLAS:
>I was thinking of the last half hour that went into making his bones and blood and now you give him mud to drink.

LADY ELDRED:
>Let Angela kiss her way through that to our lie.

>>*ROGUE's coffin becomes part of a death coach mime which wheels out into the audience. Have horse hoof sounds that differentiate between the hollow sound of a bridge and the solid roads.*

Let the audience hear bits of chain rattling on
the harness, horses whinnying. The coach is
searching for ANGELA. It has candles and lamps.
The coachman cracks his whip.

SCENE 40: THE VICARAGE VIGIL

JENNY:
>The Vicarage.

ANGELA:
>Mr. Gleneden, I can't go home. I'm afraid to go home.

GLENEDEN:
>I shall take you home to Martha. Here wait till I put
>on my cloak.

ANGELA:
>Listen! I can hear them coming over the bridge.

GLENEDEN:
>Angela, there's nothing to be afraid of.

>>*The coach comes down the second aisle and*
>>*pauses at Caresfoot Court.*

ANGELA:
>Mr. Gleneden, father sent Martha away this morning.
>There's no one at Caresfoot Court but him. He sent
>her away. She nursed my dying mother and was my
>only woman friend yet he cast her off like an old
>shoe. I tried to talk to him this afternoon but he
>just sits in the great chair in the study and stares at
>someone I can't see. Could you help me run away,
>Mr. Gleneden, and find Arthur?

GLENEDEN:
>Surely, it's not as serious as that, Angela. Ah, they've
>stopped at the Court.

ANGELA:

They're coming here now. They know where I am.

*The black coach comes up, stops. There is an
evil knock on the vicarage door. SIR EDWARD
and LADY ELDRED enter. They work together
like oily foxes.*

ANGELA:

What have you to say? Tell me quick!

LADY ELDRED:

Am I to speak before Mr. Gleneden?

ANGELA:

Yes! Speak!

LADY ELDRED:

You seem to know my news before I give it and
believe me it pains me very much to have to give it.
Angela, he is dead.

ANGELA:

I told you she would bring something evil. You're
lying. You must be. How can Arthur be dead and
I am alive? Oh for shame, it is not true. He is not
dead.

LADY ELDRED:

Do you know this ring? I took it as he asked me to
do from his dead hand that it might be given back
to you.

GLENEDEN:

If he is dead Lady Eldred, how did he die, where did
he die, and what of?

SIR EDWARD:

Sir, it was Geraldine's sad duty to nurse Arthur
Brenzaida through his last illness at Madeira. He died

106

of enteric fever. I have got a copy of his burial
certificate here which I had taken from the Portuguese
books.

ANGELA:
He is not dead.

GLENEDEN:
Angela, my love, I'm afraid you must give in to God's
will.

LADY ELDRED:
My poor Angela, why will you not believe me. Do you
suppose that Sir Edward here would want to torture
you by lying about . . . Here! I had meant to keep this
till you were calmer. But I have a letter for you. Read
it and convince yourself.

> *She gives over a letter.*

ANGELA:
Yes, this is his writing. I beg your pardon. It was good
of you to nurse him.

SIR EDWARD:
Geraldine and I did more than nurse him Angela. We,
knowing the great love you bore him, brought Mr.
Brenzaida's remains back with us to England. We have
just instructed the sexton to bury him in the Lawry
plot. There is reason for this haste.

ANGELA:
Where is he? Arthur!

> *Lantern, torches and shadows. ANGELA flies to
> the coffin and pries open the lid in mime.
> GLENEDEN drags her away.*

LADY ELDRED: *across the coffin as it is about to be
lowered into the grave* This blow comes from God,
Angela, and the religion which you believe in will

bring you consolation. Most likely it is a blessing in disguise, a thing that you will in time even learn to be thankful for.

ANGELA:
I pray God Lady Eldred that when your hour of dread comes as it will come there will be none to mock you as you mock me.

> *GLENEDEN begins the burial service. He leads ANGELA back to the vicarage. At the well, the ELDREDS and DOUGLAS drink to their success and laugh as the clock strikes twelve.*

SIR EDWARD:
Is it time to dig him up yet, Geraldine?

LADY ELDRED:
Give her one more hour to weep and then we'll scratch him up again.

> *They go to their bench, yawning and stretching.*

SCENE 41: THE EAST WIND

CHORUS:
The East Wind   The East Wind   The East Wind

The old Church tower and garden wall
Are black with autumn rain,
And dreary winds foreboding call
The darkness down again.

TABBY:
Mr. Taylor . . .

> *At Owen's bed.*

Come quickly. Owen's not well, Mrs. Taylor. Come quickly to see him.

The father and mother rush in. TABBY goes in to phone for the doctor.

MOTHER: *holding him in her arms*
Owen, it's your mother. I've brought you something to drink. Hold it, father. Help me get his mouth open.

FATHER:
We'll choke him this way.

The doctor comes down the aisle and arrives just as OWEN recovers from his fit.

OWEN:
Mother and father. It is time that you are together again. I felt you both touching me . . . Like rain. I'm not very old yet, you know. I still want to be held. If you keep on letting go of me, I'll slip away.

FATHER:
Is this delirium, doctor?

DOCTOR: *feeling OWEN's brow*
His temperature's subnormal.

He feels his pulse.

Oh for God's sake, what's the matter with you two. Why are you so artificial with each other. Go to bed together and forget all your spidery this's and that's. Make love, be one. Let me stay up with him.

They slowly withdraw.

OWEN:
Dr. Spettigue. You've shaved off the beard you were growing for me. Have we had the play then?

DOCTOR:

>No, your play's tomorrow night. Don't worry, I ordered a wonderful false beard so I can play Devil Caresfoot for you. The summer heat was too much for a real beard.

OWEN:

>You're not going to say that I can't put on the play tomorrow.

DOCTOR:

>For a moment, yes. But as I said before, Owen, live. Go to sleep now. Let me light your pipe for you. Here. Smoke one pipeful of this and then sleep Owen. Inhale as deep as ever you can. That's it. Now another. And now Owen, sleep.

>>*He tiptoes out. The foxes stand by the well looking over at ROGUE's coffin.*

SCENE 42: THE GRANGE AGAIN

JENNY:

>The Grange.

>>*ROGUE mimes being buried alive.*

LADY ELDRED:

>We will have to hurry now and scratch him up. It is just possible that he has awakened earlier than I thought.

>>*They go over and bring ROGUE out of his coffin. He walks across the stage floundering and pale.*

DOUGLAS:

>Speak up, Rogue. When I ask you a question answer me!

110

LADY ELDRED:
>We have made him mute with our tricks. I wish to
>God my own evil tongue had been torn out years ago
>but perhaps it is just as well he is mute.

>*She wipes his face with a cloth.*

>Now Douglas, you must practice at looking sick and
>dead yourself. There's not very much more time
>before young Brenzaida is back upon us. Let's hear
>how you cough.

DOUGLAS:
>Like this?

>*He coughs.*

LADY ELDRED:
>Put more rattle into it. Angela will never marry you,
>nor would I myself unless she was sure you were soon
>going to die.

CHORUS:
>>Dead, dead is my joy,
>>I long to be at rest;
>>I wish the damp earth covered
>>This desolate breast.

SCENE 43: THE BETRAYAL AND MARRIAGE

JENNY:
>The vicarage.

PIERS:
>My dear Angela, the marriage to Douglas would only
>be a form. We can get that in writing. Doctor Surrey
>says that he has not long to live. If you marry him all

the property can then be transmitted back to me and a great wrong is righted. Douglas only wants to get my land back. And marrying you Angela is the only way to get round the terms of your grandfather's will.

ANGELA:

Mr. Gleneden, what do you say?

GLENEDEN:

I've gone into all this most thoroughly Angela and what your father says is correct. It would be . . . It would have to be . . . A marriage in name only. Douglas does look extremely ill to me. He is about to die.

ANGELA:

Thank you. Alright father. If it will only end this sneaking up behind me to ask if I know this or that. As you say, it's a useful action.

PIERS:

Angela, I trusted your generosity and I was right. Now the question is . . . When?

ANGELA:

After June the ninth.

PIERS:

Angela, it has to be sooner than that. Douglas is a dying man.

ANGELA:

Tomorrow then father.

PIERS:

No, no. It will take the lawyers a month to transfer the property.

ANGELA:

> June the eighth then. Father, have you any idea why
> not the ninth?

PIERS:

> Yes, yes, I know. But Brenzaida isn't going to come
> back now. He's dead in the churchyard. Well the
> eighth it will have to be.

ANGELA:

> Get your lawyers by the way to draw up a paper for
> Douglas to sign. If he should get better our marriage
> will have to be annulled. Why do you make me think
> of all this when you must know all I really want to
> think about is my real husband who is dead.

PIERS:

> Of course, of course. Angela, you have made me a
> very happy man.

> *He embraces her and leaves.*

GLENEDEN:

> What do you see in the lake, Angela?

ANGELA:

> While I was ill I imagined that I heard the wild swans
> flying over. Are they floating on the lake now or is it
> just the sun glittering on the water? Oh Mr. Gleneden,
> my father is such a grey old wolf. I feel it in my bones.
> Look, a hair on his sleeve came off on my dress. It's
> a collie dog's hair. He's started to collect the lost dogs
> again though he knows I can't stand it.

GLENEDEN:

> Angela, let us walk down to the lake and see if the
> swans have come.

JENNY:

> At an inn in the Alps Mountains.

ARTHUR: *to someone standing up in the chorus*
Innkeeper, will these swans down on the lake stay all
summer?

INNKEEPER:
No, Herr Brenzaida. They are resting there before they
fly to the northern countries. England is one of the
countries they fly to. Will you be happy to be back in
your native country, Herr Brenzaida?

ARTHUR:
Yes, for there is someone there I love very much and
I have not seen them for a year. Angela!

JENNY:
A registry office at Roxham. Near Caresfoot Court.

> *As ARTHUR calls her name, ANGELA turns
> her head.*

CLERK:
I now declare you, Angela Caresfoot, and you, Douglas
Caresfoot, man and wife.

> *DOUGLAS coughs from his wheelchair where he
> sits bundled up and coughing. ANGELA is
> dressed in black.*

LADY ELDRED:
Let me congratulate you, Mrs. Caresfoot. Indeed I
should for I prophecied this happy event if you may
recall seven months ago.

ANGELA:
Yes, yes. Events have been too strong for me. But I'm
not really married. It's nothing but a form. Now to
be forgotten.

LADY ELDRED:
Of course Mrs. Caresfoot. Nothing but a form.

ANGELA:

Take this back. I have done with it.

She throws the ring to the floor.

LADY ELDRED:

Take this back? A married woman must wear a ring, Mrs. Caresfoot.

DOUGLAS:

Wheel me over, Edward. I must kiss my new wife.

ANGELA:

Father, don't let him touch me.

PIERS:

Not touch you, Angela. Why my dear, he is your husband.

ANGELA:

My husband! Have you all agreed to drive me mad!

LADY ELDRED whispers in DOUGLAS' ear and wheels him away. PIERS and ANGELA leave.

DOUGLAS: *standing up*

I must follow my wife.

LADY ELDRED:

Wait. First Douglas, my payment. I've done your wicked work for you and now shall have my pay.

DOUGLAS:

Leave go.

SIR EDWARD:

My dear Geraldine, it has really seemed best that I have those letters of yours.

She exclaims.

DOUGLAS:
>Why else would Sir Edward have helped us, Geraldine?
>He has to have some payment too, Geraldine. I suggest
>that this evening together you read over the letters by
>the fire and divide them among yourselves. He'll
>have favourites. So will you.

LADY ELDRED:
>Douglas, you've had a long day and now your hour
>has struck.

SIR EDWARD:
>From this moment on you are a ruined woman. A
>penniless outcast. For years I've longed to have
>revenge on you for the humilities you've made me
>suffer. And now . . .

LADY ELDRED:
>Edward, get back into the mud where you belong.
>The mud where I found you . . . A bumbling, pitiful
>little country attorney whom I made a Sir Edward.
>Douglas, there is something written on your face that
>I will some day sign with my foot!

JENNY:
>A ship at sea.

ARTHUR: *to a member of the chorus*
>There's landfall, captain. I can see the lights of the
>harbour.

CAPTAIN:
>If this storm stays off, Mr. Brenzaida. But I see the
>sunset so wild and the sky to the East so black. Aye,
>I don't think it's safe to make for port till dawn.

ANN: *crossing*
>You've no idea of what marvellous times we had playing
>out there when we were children. It was an old farm-
>house at the end of a dark lane, all shadowy. We used

to put on plays in a disused place the family called the West Room. It was our cousin who led us in dreaming it out.

CHORUS: *an individual as if in a class at a school ANN is teaching*   Did this cousin die, Miss?

> *We do hear her answer as the thunder of the storm begins.*

CHORUS:
The East Wind brings a storm. A storm!

A Storm

> *Weather vanes turning. Smoke suddenly shifting like wild blue hair from a chimney. Great armies of branches waving, creaking and groaning. A deer darts in the forest. Key holes whistling. Wires and ropes and stone walls whizzing and humming. A spider leg of branch writing and writing on a windowpane all the night through.*

Lock up your doors and pen your flocks,
  A storm comes with the night,
The stars go out and the windows latch,
  Babies cry out in fright.

Over the hills and under the sky
  The huntsman and his hounds,
The huntsman's dark and twelve feet high —
  Hear him galloping by.

His dogs gnash in their kennels of skull
  And now he lets them out,
His dogs of rage and his wolves of blood
  Raise a dreadful shout

Over the hills and under the sky
  The huntsman and his hounds.
He rides the wind with a dreadful cry
  And Hell itself comes nigh.

117

Closer they come. Have you shut the door?
 What have you left outside,
His horse must eat. Leave out a thing.
 He will not be denied.

Over the hills and under the sky
 The huntsman and his hounds —
"Have you blood for us and any bones?"
 Hear their thrilling cry!

We've left a last sheaf in the field.
 Huntsman it is for you.
Take it and leave ourselves unharmed.
 And do not us pursue.

Over the hills and under the sky
 Over the hills and under the sky
  Over the hills and under the sky
   Over the hills and under the sky.

*As sometimes in a storm, there is now a hush.
By candlelight, a huge shadow. ANGELA is
combing her hair before going to bed. Someone
has put her wedding ring on her dresser. She
looks about. DOUGLAS is hidden by the
hangings of the bed. She sees him. He comes
to her. The first thing he does is take away the
comb. Our attention now focuses on the very
first image of the play. A girl holds a small
window up to boy who taps on it with a branch.
The branch breaks the window pane. In the
storm, the Caresfoot Staff is blown down.
Perhaps there is a repeat verse of the hunting
song.*

act three

SCENE 44: BOTTLES

The scene opens with OWEN in bed.

OWEN:
Mitch, is that you talking down there?

MITCH: *emerging from the trapdoor*
Owen, I'm bringing up your batteries that you wanted for your lights.

He puts a car battery down on the forestage.

These belong to my car and I'd better get them back sometime tonight.

OWEN:
Why?

MITCH:
I want to take my girlfriend to the dan[c

OWEN:

Oh we'll be over long before the dance is over. Mitch, sit down and talk to me.

MITCH:

Will I do your favourite cartoon?

OWEN:

Yes. Now you rock in the rocking chair and I say . . .

He gets off the bed.

Grandma, how about a dime so I can get an ice cream cone and cool myself off?

MITCH:

Ah, I'll tell you a ghost story instead son. It'll freeze your bones and chill you off twice as fast. Listen!

They both go into wild laughter.

OWEN:

Mitch, you'll dig my grave and bury me, won't you?

MITCH:

No, Owen.

OWEN:

That's the part that frightens me the most. Lying out there with the others. Who'd you bury yesterday?

MITCH:

You don't lie out there. There's Heaven and all that.

OWEN:

No, there isn't. Not for a long time anyhow.

MITCH:

Don't you believe in God, Owen?

OWEN:

Sometimes. I think he's the evilest person around.

MITCH:

>You mustn't say that, Owen. He died for you on the cross.

OWEN:

>He . . . The older one didn't, Mitch. He made the tree that the cross was cut out of don't forget.

MITCH:

>Let me tell you something, Owen.

OWEN:

>You're trying to change the subject.

>*A chorus member brings over a large tray of empty bottles of all sorts and sizes.*

MITCH:

>No, I'm trying to stay on it. Do you remember, Owen, when I used to live with my granny in the old weather beaten cottage that used to be the post office when there was a village at the crossroads.

OWEN:

>Yes, and she took so much medicine.

MITCH:

>Yes, and when granny died one of the things she left me was a whole cupboard full of half empty medicine bottles.

>*He begins to sample each bottle.*

>Green bottles. Let me see what it says on the label here. The mice have chewed off some of the label here to get at the delicious mucilage. Funny little face with a Saint Andrew's cross behind it.

OWEN:

>That's a skull and crossbones, Mitch.

MITCH:
>Probably some sort of bone medicine. Yellow bottles.
>Mustard, emetic, cream of tartar, chloroform . . .

>*All of this is punctuated by faster and faster
>gulps from the bottles.*

>Sodium bicarbonate, iodine, mercurachrome, alum,
>tannic acid . . . Granny used to love her tea boiled by
>the way . . . Essence of peppermint, essence of
>digitalis, turpentine, cantharides, glycerine, molasses,
>eucalyptus, castor oil, belladonna . . . The blue
>bottles . . .

OWEN: *laughing*
>That's what they put carbolic acid in silly.

MITCH:
>Mineral oil, assafoetidae, Mecca ointment, alka-seltzer.

OWEN:
>Stop, Mitch. My stomach hurts from laughing.

MITCH:
>What I want to know is . . . Granny took all those
>medicines at one time or another and died at ninety
>when a hay wagon ran over her when she was out
>picking strawberries along the road. I finished all of
>the medicines one by one one weekend when I was
>feeling rather poorly and sort of low and had no
>money . . . What I want to know is . . . Here I am
>healthy and sound . . . How can it be after finishing
>all those medicines that there isn't a God, Owen?

>*He picks up the tray.*

OWEN:
>I believe. I believe. Mitch, can I have a blue bottle and
>a red one? And a yellow one?

MITCH: *selecting some*
>Sure.

OWEN:
>I like looking at the sun through them. Everything
>turns red. Everything turns yellow.
>
>*He looks through the bottles.*
>
>Everything turns blue . . . Blue as tonight when we put
>on the play.
>
>*The stage turns all these colours. As it turns blue,
>the chorus enter as the audience for the play.
>They come down the aisle and JENNY steps
>forward.*

JENNY:
>The road. June the ninth. The road to Caresfoot
>Court.

SCENES 45, 46 & 47:
THE ROAD TO CARESFOOT COURT

ARTHUR:
>Did you see Angela Caresfoot then?

OSTLER:
>Law, yes sir, that I have. I saw her yesterday morning
>driving through the Roxham market place with her
>father.

ARTHUR:
>How did she look?

OSTLER:
>A bit pale I thought, sir. But well enough. And
>wonderful handsome. You'll have to take the road
>round the forest, sir, if you're going to Caresfoot
>Court. There's a great tree fallen across this road
>with last night's storm and they say the Caresfoot
>Staff is down.

He goes from stage left to stage right.

The road leads ARTHUR closer to the well. In the forest (chorus), he meets MARTHA.

ANGELA sits brooding by the fallen step ladder and the haunted well.

DOUGLAS and LADY ELDRED loom separately in the background.

ARTHUR:

Martha, what are you doing on this side of the village? Have you left Caresfoot Court?

MARTHA:

Mr. Brenzaida! What has brought you back and why do you come to me? I never wronged you.

ARTHUR:

What are you talking about? I have come to marry Angela. We are going to be married today.

MARTHA:

It is really *you*, sir! And she married yesterday . . . Oh God!

ARTHUR:

Don't laugh at me, Martha, please don't laugh. Why do you shake so? What do you mean?

MARTHA:

Mean! I mean that my Angela married her cousin Douglas Caresfoot at Roxham yesterday. Heaven forgive me for having to tell it to you!

Have the deer antler image come in here. ARTHUR runs through the forest. On the lake spread with a blue cloth sits a swan. ARTHUR breaks its neck with a stick, then he comes upon ANGELA dressed in black sitting by the well. She holds her doll. Keeper barks at him.

ANGELA:

There Keeper. Don't keep thinking your master will
come up the road. He never will again.

ARTHUR:

Angela, is this true? Are you married?

ANGELA:

Oh Arthur, my darling. You have come back to me.
Am I dead or alive? I am dead then. Is it really you?
Alas, yes, I am married. But Arthur . . .

ARTHUR:

Get back! Don't dare to touch me! Do you know
what you are? Fresh from your husband's arms and
ready to throw yourself into mine! Shame upon you!
Were you married yesterday?

ANGELA:

Oh Arthur, have pity! Merciful God, make him
understand! Wait! Wait!

ARTHUR:

Don't kneel to me. Get up!

ANGELA:

The ring, Arthur! How did they get it away from
you?

ARTHUR:

I sent it back to show you I was still true to you. If it
meant otherwise would I not write and break the
promise to your father? Was your lust for your cousin
so strong that you could not wait till after I returned?
When I think of the temptation I withstood . . . And I
am a man. An older woman constantly by me dreaming of my flesh. I swear night after night until I
could stand it no longer. I took ship for Europe where
I wandered over mountains and through southern
valleys slowly towards the snow I knew waited for me
here. But I see now that you were weaker than I and
bubbled in March, no, in January, like tar on a

scorched July highway. My mistress of pitch, go back
to the animal you prefer to me. Tell him those are
tears of happiness and let him kiss them quite away.

He flings her off.

DOUGLAS:
Leave the girl be! If you really loved her you'd never
have left her, you fool.

He picks up a stone.

You're the one who killed my dog and laughed when
I tripped over the footstool at Lady Eldred's.

ARTHUR:
Yes, I am. Put that down and fight fair.

He backs up to edge of well.

DOUGLAS:
You fight fair then. Call off that brute of a dog!

ARTHUR:
Get Angela to call him off. She's your wife and should
take your orders. I don't want to see either of you
dreadful pair ever again. And when I marry, Angela,
I shall have the grace to let you know.

He leaves.

Poor girl, I guess you could not help it. Your father
played a similar trick on my mother.

ANGELA:
Arthur! Help me!

*The dog springs and topples DOUGLAS over
into the well. He hangs on to the edge of the
well but LADY ELDRED runs up and standing
on the edge of the well stamps on his hands
until he lets go and howling falls with Keeper*

deep into the earth. The whole chorus leap up
and go over to the well to see what has
happened.

LADY ELDRED:
That rather evens the score between us, Douglas.
Now for the other one.

She disappears.

GLENEDEN and PIERS appear.

Becoming dogs, the chorus slink down the
aisles and gather in a tight little group waiting
for their signal.

ANGELA:
Then let me follow this husband of mine.

They hold her back until she turns on her father.

You Judas who sold me. They bought the use of me
from you for a year, didn't they, Judas? And when
they had duped me good and properly then you got
your title and the land back. Squire Caresfoot, Squire
Judas.

PIERS slowly withdraws to his chair where he
sits staring at the ghost of CLAUDIA.

Oh Mr. Gleneden, I am betrayed! They tricked you
but I am most betrayed! Arthur still lives and was
here. It's so dark! Lead me to Martha beyond the
forest, someplace in the past when I was still. The doll
looks at me! Now I know why she gave it to me. So I
would have something when she had stripped away
everything and everyone else.

DR. SURREY:
Get her up to her bed. We'll have to tie her down.
She's too violent.

ANGELA:

>Oh good Doctor Surrey. Was Douglas so ill these past few months? I am a better doctor than you are. I cured him with but a night's nursing and all his teeth and claws and thorns were good as new by dawn.

>*They tie her to her bed.*

>Is this the way Doctor Surrey you and your students tie the poor dogs down before you cut them up alive in your amphitheatre?

DR. SURREY:

>Pay no attention to her. Run and get her old nurse Martha and bring some more rope. She's broken through this and I can't hold her down much longer.

ANGELA:

>My father has some more dogs ready for you, good Doctor Surrey. After you have secured me I would go and sample them. Some sweet little terriers and adorable spaniels! And perchance among them one mongrel boarshound with your face!

>*PIERS stares at CLAUDIA's ghost.*

CLAUDIA:

>I'll come when thou art saddest,
>Laid alone in the darkened room;
>When the mad day's mirth has vanished,
>And the smile of joy is banished
>From evening's chilly gloom.

>*A bell tolls.*

>Listen, 'tis just the hour,
>The awful time for thee;
>Dost thou not feel upon thy soul
>A flood of strange sensations roll,
>Forerunners of a sterner power,
>Heralds of me?

PIERS:

Claudia, don't come any closer to me. Don't look at me like that.

CLAUDIA:

Piers Caresfoot, you have broken the vow you made to me to look after our child. You have sold her for money like an animal! Hear my revenge! My teeth are sharpened with the North Wind of Hunger. My tongue is parched and famished with the East Wind of Hate. I shall slake my hunger and thirst upon you until people will ask where you were and find only the palms of your hands.

PIERS:

I haven't fed them. They're hungry in their kennels. If I could just rise I could leave this room and feed them.

CLAUDIA:

It saves money not to feed them. We met because you saved money by taking a second class ticket.

PIERS:

Why can't I rise?

CLAUDIA:

A year ago Piers, you sold your feet. Remember? You sold your feet up to your thighs. That is why you'll never rise from that chair again.

LADY ELDRED and ROGUE enter with a rope. They tie PIERS to his chair.

LADY ELDRED:

Well Squire Caresfoot, long ago your father told the village constable to whip my father out of the village. He died in a ditch that night. I, his poor daughter by. Now it's time the Caresfoots paid all of their debt to the Almedas. Oh you are worse than I am. I bit and scratched to save my life. But you sold a beautiful

young girl to get back your clay. I knew you'd do it.
And now that you've done it I know I must kill you
for it. Like the Christians' God I tempt and if you
fall, I destroy. Put your thumb on this knot, Rogue.
Squire Caresfoot, the fifty starving dogs you were
going to hand over to that scientific fiend are waiting
in their pens for a supper that never comes. We'll
leave the door ajar. And if they don't smell you out
as we leap to safety then they deserve to starve. But
there's one dog, a great black one that knows his
carrion master!

> *LADY ELDRED and ROGUE disappear. After
> some seconds of silence, we hear a faint barking far
> away. A faint scream. Then a great big black dog
> bounds across the stage and knocks PIERS over
> in his chair.*

> *The chorus rush up and carry PIERS away, chair
> and all. The stage is now divided between
> ANGELA on stage right in the bed and LADY
> ELDRED on stage left in the wheelchair.*

LADY ELDRED:
Rogue, light a candle and bring it to me. Thank you.
Stand there.

> *She burns a paper at the candle.*

I might have given this talisman of my power to Angela
if she could have sworn never to continue her love for
that wretched weakling, Arthur Brenzaida. But I know
how loving and weak her heart is. Rogue, bring me a
glass of red wine.

> *From a secret box she takes a small vial.*

Ah, stars who look down on me and this poor clown.
Evil winking Algol, clearest Aldebaran, and blood red
Antares in Scorpio in a moment I shall find myself in
your depths or in the mind behind you or far beyond.

She pours the vial into the wine which boils up furiously.

Once long ago, I cradled an old man's silver locks and swore I would topple the chimneys of Caresfoot Court. Its master lies devoured and chewed by his own hounds. Once long ago, I swore I would break into their houses. Now I have slaked my thirst in the wine cellars of their hearts and pantries of their bones.

She drinks.

In my cloak I walk through the forest beneath the moon and the coursing cloud shadows to find you my scattered child and take you home again . . . My lost child, my bonny nursling, your cradle floats in the tempest of my starless night.

She falls, struggles to her knees, then falls again. Suddenly, she is OWEN's mother.

OWEN: *talking to his mother at extreme forestage*
Mother, thank you so much for being in my play. And for coming out when you saw the posters.

MOTHER:
I wouldn't have missed being in your play for worlds, Owen. That silly old story has been a favourite of mine ever since I was sixteen.

OWEN:
When father gave it to you.

MOTHER:
When your father gave it to me.

OWEN:
What are you going to do now, mother?

MOTHER:
I don't know, Owen. What do you want me to do?

OWEN: *pause*

>I'll be very good and go to sleep almost instantly if you promise me one thing. Mother, stay here with us. Stay with father and me. Don't run off with him.

MOTHER:

>Why Owen, yes. If you go to sleep almost instantly. Yes, I promise I will stay.

>*She takes him to his bed and tucks him in.*

>Good night, Owen.

OWEN:

>Good night, mother.

>*When she returns to the forestage, the father is there waiting for her.*

FATHER:

>Are you going to stay?

MOTHER:

>Don't be silly. Of course not. Surely you don't want me to stay.

FATHER:

>You're going to ride off now on my best horse.

MOTHER:

>Of course. Try and stop me. That horse obeys my whistle and not yours. By the way could you tell Owen to keep cutting off those thorns on the locust trees in the orchard. The little colts can kill themselves if they get pressed against them.

FATHER:

>I want you to stay. Tonight. Owen . . . I have a feeling . . . That he'll go tonight.

MOTHER:
>I can't stand sickness and death. You gave me two children who died.

FATHER:
>As I've said before woman, when I was his age I had these attacks too. When the crisis came, I called for my mother. She held me in her arms for a day and a night. By the next morning I was better.

MOTHER:
>And she crawled off to die no doubt. No . . . Sorry. I'm off. Goodbye.

FATHER:
>But what if he calls for you.

>>*There is no answer, only hoof beats as GERALDINE rides away.*

OWEN:
>Father.

FATHER: *advancing to the bed*
>Yes, Owen.

OWEN:
>I hear a horse galloping away. Is that mother?

FATHER:
>No, Owen. Only a horse galloping away in the pasture.

OWEN:
>Where is mother then?

FATHER:
>Upstairs.

OWEN:
>Do you know father, I've been thinking. I don't think I should have ended my play with Angela dying and Geraldine lingering on.

FATHER:

How should you have ended it? I'd like the part changed where I tie Angela to the bed. And I also feel that Mitch shouldn't get eaten up by those dogs.

OWEN:

Oh no, I couldn't change that. But I'd like to go on like this . . .

ANGELA resumes her position on the bed.

I want it to be winter. Snow is falling. Angela has recovered and lies in the Red Room at Caresfoot Court.

SCENE 48: SNOW

Snow falls. OWEN ladles it out from up on the stepladder.

ANGELA:

Martha, can I reach out and touch the snowflake?

MARTHA:

You're not tied down anymore, Miss Angela.

ANGELA:

All the snow is falling into the puddle of blood. Lady Eldred, ah there you are, I've caught you. You won't fall yet. You'll stay on my sleeve a while yet. My arm is cold enough to keep you still hexagonal. Listen to that fly buzzing, Martha. Ah, he's happy and content from the heat of the fire. There's my father. I'll let you fall. You've wanted to fall into the puddle of blood for a long time. Ah, Douglas. You shoot fast down, don't you? Has he floated down the stream into the lake yet, Martha? The cattle and deer will not drink at that well for a good many months to come,

will they? Ah there's my snowflake. No, don't fall
yet. There's another little snowflake with you. Don't
let that one fall, Martha. Why it's broad daylight.
Have I been ill and dreaming like that long, Martha.
What time of year is it?

MARTHA:

December, Miss Angela. It's deep snow out of doors.

ANGELA:

I dreamt something about Lady Eldred. Was it something true?

MARTHA:

Ah, miss. Are you well enough for me to tell you?
She tried to take her life. Poor dreadful woman. The
poison she took only paralyzed all her limbs. She is
wheeled about in a wheelchair by Rogue and although
she can think and speak she does not speak but at
night asks to be wheeled to an eastern window where
she can stare at a certain evil winking star.

ANGELA:

Now I know that star. It is the tooth of Medusa's
Head which Perseus holds. My whole life has been
spent beneath its influence. Which of the twelve winds
of Heaven shall blow it out? The West Wind! The
West Wind! Oh come and help me free the prisoner,
the river frozen in the jail of winter.

A messenger of Hope, comes every night to me,
And offers for short life, eternal liberty.
He comes with western winds, with evening's wandering airs
With that clear dusk of heaven that brings the thickest stars;
Winds take a pensive tone, and stars a tender fire,
And visions rise and change which kill me with desire —

Bring me the doll, Martha. The doll that she gave me
so long ago.

LADY ELDRED: *wheeled in on other side of stage by*
        ROGUE   Stop all the clocks. All the clocks in the
        house, doctor. I cannot bear any repetitive sound.
        Even the intake of my breath is like a dreadful puffing
        nostrilled tube-clock that gives me almost enough
        strength to hold my breath. But no, I must go on
        breathing.

DR. SURREY:
        Is there anything further you would wish, Lady
        Eldred?

LADY ELDRED:
        I wish to die. Don't you understand, you vivisecting
        fool. Kill me. I want death?

GHOST:
        Evil mother. Cruel murderess. I speak from beneath
        the snow. Your wish is granted. You've been a wolf
        in the forest twice times seven years and now you will
        be freed . . .

        ANGELA kisses the doll.

        For at last someone good enough has been found to
        kiss the rag doll you made of my bones, loving enough
        to lick the sores of Lazarus, and gentle enough to weep
        for the scorpion. Farewell. I have found at last my
        true mother. The West Wind blows and lights the
        Evening Star.

DR. SURREY:
        Wheel her to her room, Rogue. Your mistress, she is
        dead.

ANGELA:
        Martha, what's that music I keep hearing?

MARTHA:
        You have sharp ears, Miss Angela. It's the musicians

practicing up for the grand ball that's to be given tonight at Hawkscliffe Hall.

ANGELA:
Has Arthur come back then?

MARTHA:
Aye, Miss. He says he's going to be married. He'll announce his betrothal tonight.

ANGELA: *turning away*
Whom is he marrying?

MARTHA:
I have no idea, Miss Angela. Why don't you open your invitation and see if he says.

She gives letter which ANGELA does not open.

ANGELA:
Was he cruel enough to invite me? As for that, I am cruel enough to accept.

MARTHA:
Here is a ball dress I've had made for you. Put it on. But wear over it this russet cloak to keep you warm.

ANGELA:
This cloak's an ugly old thing, Martha.

MARTHA:
We're not rich enough for both a new cloak and a new dress, Miss Angela.

ANGELA:
How are we to get to Arthur's place through all this deep snow, Martha?

MARTHA:
Ah, I've a horse called the West Wind and a sleigh. Get in and I'll drive.

Sleigh bells.

ANGELA:

Go fast through the forest, Martha. There's a white wolf after us.

MARTHA:

No, it's the moon skating along over the snow drifts beside us.

ANGELA:

We've got a head start!

The sleigh goes over the bridge.

SCENE 49: THE BALL

The three girl cousins and OWEN walk to the front of the stage with four small chairs in their hands which they set down in front of them. Huge shadows are cast behind them. They are free in Eternity. They will never taste death again.

We wove a web in childhood
    A web of sunny air;
We dug a spring in infancy
    Of water pure and fair;

We sowed in youth a mustard seed,
    We cut an almond rod;
We are now grown up to ripened age;
    Are they withered in the sod?

The mustard seed in distant land
    Bends down a mighty tree;
The dry, unbudding almond wand
    Has touched eternity.

But the spring was under a mossy stone,
    Its jet may gush no more;
Hark, skeptic, bid thy doubts be gone;
    Is that a feeble roar?

Rushing around thee, lo! The tide
    Of waves where armed fleets may ride,
Sinking and swelling, frowns and smiles,
    An ocean with a thousand isles
    And scarce a glimpse of shore.

JENNY:

    I want to ask you a favour. In "The Saga of Caresfoot Court," I want Angela not to die. I want her to live.

OWEN:

    Well Jenny, I must confess when we drew the straws to see whether she would live or die I tipped the death one your way ever so slightly. But I've already decided to end it a new way.

JENNY:

    Then listen to the West Wind and how it finished the tale!

OWEN:

    Hawkscliffe Hall. The West Wind.

    The dancers at ARTHUR's place. At first they dance to the tune the fiddler played on the village green. ANGELA enters. The dancers stop. ARTHUR advances to meet her and there is a hush.

ANGELA:

    Arthur Brenzaida, you have invited me this evening to meet your new bride. I have put off my mourning to come and I cannot stay long. Where is your new bride?

ARTHUR:

Angela, I have not had to bring my new bride with
me.

ANGELA:

Why not?

ARTHUR:

My darling, she has come to dance with me by herself.

*He takes off her cloak and dances with her. At
first she hides her face, but slowly revives her past
assurance with him. The dance continues and the
giant shadows of the four genii lean over the
dawn they have made.*

production notes

Five years ago, I saw the Peking National Opera perform a centuries old play, *At the Fairy Mountain Bridge*. The orchestra sat on stage. Gestures and mime took the place of props and sets. I remember a fabulous boat just made by two actors pretending. Art is made by subtracting from reality and letting the viewer imagine or "dream it out," as Owen is told to in the play.

Four years ago, John Hirsch directed one of my children's plays, *Names and Nicknames*, at the Manitoba Theatre Centre. With a dozen children, six young actors (among them, Martha Henry and Heath Lambert), and words taken from my father's old *Practical Speller*, John Hirsch created a magic hour that has remained with me ever since. The simpler art is, the richer it is. Words, gestures, a few rhythm band instruments create a world that turns Cinerama around and makes you the movie projector.

I watched the kids playing around our verandah. On a primitive skateboard they roll Malcolm, aged three, about and say, "You're a turkey. Now we'll put you in the oven."

We've had theatre of cruelty (the rebirth of tragedy — the imitation of our deathwish); we've had theatre of the absurd (the rebirth of comedy — the imitation of our bitter laughter); we've had the theatre of detachment (the rebirth of the miracle play — Mother Courage drags her cross). The one thing we never imitate enough is games, play . . . imitation itself, the instinct just to "have fun," to make a pattern simply because, like a whooping crane, we can't help doing a spring dance with our bodies. Look at kids playing hopscotch.

When I was eight, one of my favourite books was Rider Haggard's *Dawn*. It's a melodrama but it still affects me very powerfully because the patterns in it are not only sensational, but deadly accurate. This is a world. Give into its rules a bit, and you'll find that it guides you out of the abyss we live in a bit more quickly than some dramas I could name (Read *Alphabet* No. 10, where one of Canada's most promising young poets analyzes Haggard's novels in the light of my comments here. My play is about young people who put on Rider Haggard's *Dawn* because of its strong pattern).

I hope that out of what you see in *Listen to the Wind*, a new theatre in Canada might grow — a theatre that has time, thinking, and the beginnings of a national tradition behind it (Read *Alphabet* No. 4, for an editorial on Canadian Theatre).

The play within the play must *not* be played for laughs. It undoubtedly will receive some, particularly Geraldine's remark after hurtling Douglas down the well. What the reader and director should try to see is that Owen does not find the story laughable. To him and to his friends, it is very, very real. Once you play it this way, the story takes over, becomes a symbol of a mind in which being betrayed and heartlessly manipulated are like an illness, like a desertion. Owen's long speech about Angela's perfidy needs cutting — cut to the capabilities of the actor. In production, try for as much fluidity as possible. Like a river. For example, in Scene 13, the boy who will carry the coach wheel should start to get it from where it is leaning on the prop table at the end of the second last verse of the song. Maria Lawry should be ready to get into the "coach" by the last lines of the song, in effect, a "dissolve."

Warning: The play is *long*. The first act is 45 minutes; the second act, 55 minutes; the third act, 30 minutes, O.k. Help us make a possible beginning for something new and very much our own — listen to the wind. It's long, o.k., but so is the wind.

Colours in the Dark — James Reaney
The Ecstasy of Rita Joe — George Ryga
Captives of the Faceless Drummer — George Ryga
Crabdance — Beverley Simons
Listen to the Wind — James Reaney
Esker Mike & His Wife, Agiluk — Herschel Hardin
Sunrise on Sarah — George Ryga
Walsh — Sharon Pollock
The Factory Lab Anthology — Connie Brissenden, ed.
Battering Ram — David Freeman
Hosanna — Michel Tremblay
Les Belles Soeurs — Michel Tremblay
API 2967 — Robert Gurik
You're Gonna Be Alright Jamie Boy — David Freeman
Bethune — Rod Langley
Preparing — Beverley Simons
Forever Yours Marie-Lou — Michel Tremblay
En Pièces Détachées — Michel Tremblay
Lulu Street — Ann Henry
Three Plays by Eric Nicol — Eric Nicol
Fifteen Miles of Broken Glass — Tom Hendry
Bonjour, là, Bonjour — Michel Tremblay
Jacob's Wake — Michael Cook
On the Job — David Fennario
Sqrieux-de-Dieu — Betty Lambert
Some Angry Summer Songs — John Herbert
The Execution — Marie-Claire Blais
Tiln & Other Plays — Michael Cook
The Great Wave of Civilization — Herschel Hardin
La Duchesse de Langeais & Other Plays — Michel Tremblay
Have — Julius Hay
Cruel Tears — Ken Mitchell and Humphrey & the Dumptrucks
Ploughmen of the Glacier — George Ryga
Nothing to Lose — David Fennario
Les Canadiens — Rick Salutin
Seven Hours to Sundown — George Ryga
Can You See Me Yet? — Timothy Findley
Two Plays — George Woodcock
Ashes — David Rudkin
Spratt — Joe Wiesenfeld
Walls — Christian Bruyere
Boiler Room Suite — Rex Deverell
Angel City, Curse of the Starving Class & Other Plays — Sam Shepard
Mackerel — Israel Horovitz
Buried Child & Other Plays — Sam Shepard
The Primary English Class — Israel Horovitz
Jitters — David French
Balconville — David Fennario
Aléola — Gaëtan Charlebois
After Abraham — Ron Chudley
Sainte-Marie Among the Hurons — James W. Nichol

The Lionel Touch — George Hulme
The Twilight Dinner & Other Plays — Lennox Brown

TALONBOOKS — THEATRE FOR THE YOUNG

Raft Baby — Dennis Foon
The Windigo — Dennis Foon
Heracles — Dennis Foon
A Chain of Words — Irene Watts
Apple Butter — James Reaney
Geography Match — James Reaney
Names and Nicknames — James Reaney
Ignoramus — James Reaney
A Teacher's Guide to Theatre for Young People — Jane Baker
A Mirror of Our Dreams — Joyce Doolittle and Zina Barnieh